THE
SCENTED
CHRISTMAS

THE SCENTED CHRISTMAS

FRAGRANT DECORATIONS, GIFTS AND CARDS FOR THE FESTIVE SEASON

GAIL DUFF

Illustrated by ANTONIA ENTHOVEN

RODALE PRESS, EMMAUS, PENNSYLVANIA

Published in the United States of America by
Rodale Press, Inc.
33 East Minor Street, Emmaus, Pennsylvania 18098

Conceived and produced by Breslich & Foss
Golden House, 28-31 Great Pulteney Street
London W1R 3DD

Designed by Peartree Design Associates
Typeset by Angel Graphics

Design and Typesetting © 1991 Breslich & Foss
Illustrations © 1991 Antonia Enthoven
Text © 1991 Gail Duff

Manufactured in Singapore

If you have any questions or comments concerning this book,
please write:
Rodale Press
Book Reader Service
33 East Minor Street
Emmaus, PA 18098

Library of Congress Cataloging-in-Publication Data

Duff, Gail
The scented Christmas/by Gail Duff.
p.   cm.
ISBN 0-87857-974-5 hardcover
1. Christmas decorations. 2. Potpourris (Scented floral mixtures)
I. Title.
TT900.C4D84 1991   91-6494
745.594'12--dc20   CIP

Distributed in the book trade by St. Martin's Press

2   4   6   8   10   9   7   5   3   hardcover

CONTENTS

Introduction 6

Author's Note 9

INTRODUCTION

Christmas is a special time of year – a time when we decorate the house, prepare wonderful food, enjoy giving and once again celebrate the coming of light into the world. We hear the melodies of the carols, enjoy looking at Christmas lights and decorations and also, although we may not realize it, appreciate the different scents associated with this time.

How often have you caught a fleeting waft of a scent and thought, 'That reminds me of Christmas!' It might have been your uncle's cigar, incense in a church, a particular kind of soap that a friend always gives you, the smell of tangerines in the fruit bowl or even the sage that you put into the stuffing. Then there is the piny scent of the tree, the burning of those special apple logs that you always reserve for Christmas day or the warming smell of the punch that greets you when you arrive at a party. Yes, Christmas is certainly a time of scents even before you begin to make your own.

Christmas scents have always been natural and, as such, never overpowering, so whether you are making your own decorations or a gift for a friend, you must try to use scents that complement them, not take them over. Never make anything that is really strongly scented or it will fill the whole house and end up being unpleasant. Scented decorations should be scattered around the house so that the tantalizing hints wafting from several directions combine to create a pleasant background.

If you want to make your Christmas a scented one, where do you begin? If the idea is to make only one or two things, then you can safely leave this until the beginning of December, although it is worth while looking around the shops in October as soon as the best materials arrive. If you make your decorations and gifts well ahead of the day and have the time to put a bit of yourself into them, the whole exercise becomes much more personal. Children will also enjoy making or helping to make gifts for relatives and friends.

So, what can you make for Christmas that is scented? The following pages are divided into three sections: decorations for the house, decorations for tree and table, and cards and gifts.

Many of the house decorations make use of fresh evergreens. They bring their own scent into the house and look wonderful without much effort on your part. You can weave them into garlands or wreaths, or use them as decorations for the stairs. Other arrangements make use of dried flowers and these can be kept for several years. Others need fabric and ribbons, while the

pomanders are made from fruits. Many items are filled with a mixture called 'Christmas spicery', a name with a lovely medieval sound and a scent that is a combination of freshness and warm spices.

The tree decorations also make use of this mixture. They are simple to construct and look as good as any bought baubles.

The decorations for the table have their own special scent, using rosemary and bay which complement the scents and tastes of Christmas food. There are napkin rings, place names and centrepieces that go well together but which can also be used alone.

Personalized gifts are always a pleasure to give or receive. Cards, gift tags, bags and baskets can all be filled with scents that match the personality of the receiver. Bath oils, colognes and talcum powder are cheap and simple to make and again you can mix and match your scents.

You can have great fun making up the different-shaped containers for the various kits of herbs and spices. There are pretty drawstring bags for potpourri and amusing pie- and pudding-shaped containers for the cooking herb spices.

How many you make is up to you. Never take on too much and end up in a panic having to work all night just two days before the family arrive on Christmas Eve. That is not the idea at all. Enjoy what you do, give yourself time, and if you find you cannot get everything done, just remind yourself to start earlier next year.

When you put up a scented garland or hang decorations on a tree, it is wonderful to see the transformation of the house and to know you helped bring it about.

Lastly, there is the ultimate pleasure of watching someone open a card or a gift and hearing them say, 'How marvellous! I've never seen one of these before.' Then you know, that in making your Christmas a scented one, you have given pleasure both to yourself and to other people.

AUTHOR'S NOTE

The special materials and ingredients required to make each item are listed throughout the book. Where alternatives are given you should choose whichever is more familiar and/or available. Other commonplace tools and pieces of equipment will also be necessary. You will require needles, thread in various colours, pins, scissors, dress-maker's chalk, a measuring tape, a sewing machine, a pencil, pen, craft knife, iron, small paintbrush, scrap paper and common kitchen equipment.

The imperial and metric measurements should not be used interchangeably. Due to the limitations of space, the patterns on pages 114-17 are drawn at one third of their actual size. A grid is provided so that you can make the required enlargement on a piece of graph paper in order to make your own pattern or template.

DECK THE HALLS

Wreaths on the door, garlands around the sitting room, clusters of pine cones hanging everywhere and blazing fires all help to make Christmas special. If these can all be scented as well, your house will be filled with tantalizing, spicy scents for the entire twelve days of Christmas.

The excitement of the season can begin on the first of December with the opening of the first window or drawer of your Advent calendar. Inside the calendar there can be a different scent for each day; when they are all put together they will make a special potpourri or rope of spices for Christmas.

Garlands and wreaths of fresh evergreen branches are always a pleasure to make, but if you do not have a good supply of fresh greenery you can use dried flowers or even make garlands from fabric. You can also buy ready-made wreaths and add scented decorations.

Advent Potpourri

Open a drawer in a decorated box every day in December and gradually build up a Christmas potpourri. Keep the box for yourself or make it as a special Advent gift. It can be refilled every year.

CALENDAR

24 matchboxes
$2 \times 1\frac{1}{4}$ in (5×3.5 cm)

•

glue for card and fabric

•

24 pieces of thin
Christmas-print fabric
$2\frac{1}{4} \times 1\frac{3}{4}$ in (5.5×4.5 cm)

•

1 piece of Christmas-print
fabric $7\frac{1}{2} \times 6$ in
(19×15 cm)

1 piece of Christmas-print
fabric $16\frac{1}{2} \times 3\frac{1}{2}$ in
(42×9 cm)

•

24 split-pin paper
fasteners

•

1 piece of thin white
card to form the base of
the drawers

FILLINGS FOR BOXES

$\frac{3}{4}$ oz (22 g) bay leaves,
roughly crumbled

•

$\frac{1}{2}$ oz (15 g) rosemary

•

$\frac{1}{2}$ oz (15 g) hibiscus
flowers

•

3 pine cones,
broken into segments

•

1 oz (30 g) cloves

•

1 oz (30 g) juniper berries

$\frac{1}{2}$ oz (15 g) cinnamon
sticks, broken

•

$\frac{1}{2}$ oz (15 g) orris root
powder

•

lemon oil

•

clove oil

•

rosemary oil

•

orange oil

Lay four of the matchboxes side by side on the table, all facing the same way. Glue them together. Glue another four boxes together and place them on top of the first four, putting glue on the top and bottom of the boxes. Continue until you have a set of drawers six boxes high. Leave the glue to dry completely.

Take out one drawer. Apply glue on the inside and outside of one end wall, including about $\frac{1}{2}$ in (1.3 cm) of the sides at that end, inside and out, and about $\frac{5}{8}$ in (1.3 cm) of the base. Place the glued end of the drawer on the centre of one of the small rectangles of fabric. Stick the sides of the fabric to the sides of the drawer. Trim into the top corners and fold in the excess fabric. Fold the excess fabric under at the bottom and trim off the corners. Leave the drawer to dry and repeat with all of the rest. Insert a paper fastener into the centre of the covered end of each drawer.

Cover the back of the set of matchbox drawers with the

left-hand corner and working from left to right along each row. Put the contents of the first drawer into a plastic bag. Add the contents of the succeeding drawers to it, crushing the spices.' Glue the card to base of the boxes.

Fill the drawers as follows:
1/2/3 – Bay leaves plus 1 drop of lemon oil.
4/5/6 – Bay leaves plus 1 drop of clove oil.
7/8 – Rosemary plus 1 drop of rosemary oil.
9/10 – Rosemary plus 1 drop each of rosemary and orange oil.
11/12/13 – Hibiscus.
14/15 – Pine cones.
16/17/18 – Cloves.
19/20/21 – Juniper.
22/23 – Cinnamon.
24 – Orris root powder.

Alternative method: the drawers can be made up in rows of two boxes only to make them tall and thin. In this case, sew a loop of the same Christmas-print fabric on the back so that the potpourri can hang on a wall.

$7\frac{1}{2} \times 6$-in (19 × 15 cm) piece of fabric, gluing it only to the sides, base and top. On one long side of the remaining piece of fabric fold over and glue a $\frac{5}{8}$ in (1.3 cm) seam allowance. Check the fabric for width (it should equal that of the top and sides of the drawers) and fold over and glue the other side to make it fit. Glue the prepared piece of fabric over the top and sides of the drawers, folding over the excess fabric at the base.

If the drawers are a gift, write the following instructions on the card: 'Open one drawer each day, beginning at the top

ADVENT CALENDAR

This is an Advent calendar with a difference in that here the pictures are on the outside of the doors. Behind the doors are cut-out shapes concealing a mixture of herbs and spices. As each door is opened, the scent increases.

CALENDAR

2 pieces of white card,
12 × 20 in (30 × 51 cm)
•
1 piece of thick dark blue
paper 12 × 20 in
(30 × 51 cm)
•
1 piece of thin green card
12 × 20 in (5 × 30 cm)
•
glue
•
24 pictures from old
Christmas cards
•
24 split-pin paper fasteners

gold and silver stick-on stars
(optional)
•
inside drawers of
24 2 × 1¼ in (5 × 3.5 cm)
matchboxes
•
23 pieces of silver fabric
3 × 2½ in (7.5 × 6 cm)
•
1 piece of gold fabric
3 × 2½ in (7.5 × 6 cm)
•
masking tape
•
Blu-Tack or similar
adhesive for fixing to
the wall

FILLING

1 oz (25 g) bay leaves,
crumbled
•
1 oz (25 g) rosemary
•
1 oz (25 g) cloves, crushed

1 oz (25 g) juniper
berries, crushed
•
1 oz (25 g) cinnamon
sticks, crushed
•
3 drops each of clove, lemon,
orange and rosemary oil

On one piece of white card, draw rectangles the same size as the matchbox drawers, equally spaced and with a margin of 1½ in (4 cm) around the edge. Using a craft knife, cut out these rectangles. Lay the cut-out white card on the blue paper and draw round the outline of each rectangle. Do the same on the green card.

Trace and cut out the shapes on pages 118-19 of the angel, bell, holly, moon, tree, stocking and star. Trace the shapes onto the rectangles on the blue paper, repeating the first six three times and the fourth time replacing the stocking with the star on the bottom right-hand corner. Using a craft knife, cut the shapes out of the blue paper. Glue the blue paper onto the white card so that the cut-out shapes correspond with the cut-out rectangles.

Cut out a template for the doors, using the shape given on page 118. Lay this template over the picture on one of the old Christmas cards and draw round it. Cut out the shape

from the card. Do the same with the other 23 cards.

Glue the cut-out pictures onto the marked rectangles on the green card. Leave them to dry completely. Push the paper fasteners through the pictures to make handles. With the point of a pair of scissors, score down the left-hand side of each door. Run a craft knife around the other edges, but do not press out the doors. Glue the green card over the blue paper, matching the doors to the cut-out shapes and rectangles.

Mix the ingredients for the filling together and fill each matchbox drawer. Lay a piece of fabric over the filling and glue it to the sides of the box, trimming the corners. When the glue is dry, use masking tape to secure the boxes to the under-side of the first piece of white card, with the fabric against the cut-out shapes. Make sure the gold box is put against the star of the last door. Glue the second piece of white card over the back of the boxes to give a tidy appearance.

Scented Holly and Ivy Wreath

A wreath of evergreens hanging on the door is always a welcoming sight. Make it scented and its warm, spicy fragrance will give pleasure whenever the door is opened. Because of its fabric centre, this wreath is best hung on a door that is protected by a porchway, or on an inside door.

MATERIALS

1 wire coat hanger

damp sphagnum moss

reel of rose or floral wire

stub wire or floral pins

holly and ivy branches –
8 of the holly branches
should be about 15 in
(38 cm) long and flexible,
the rest can be shorter

2 circles of red printed
fabric, each 9¼ in (23.5 cm)
in diameter

8 holly-leaf shapes cut from
plain green fabric
(see page 119)

glue for fabric

8 pieces of red bias binding,
each 3 in (7.5 cm) long

8 in (20 cm) of ½-in-wide
(1.3 cm) red ribbon

2 yd (1.8 m) of 2-in-wide
(5 cm) red ribbon

'Christmas spicery'
(page 114)

Bend the coat hanger into a circle, keeping the hook in shape. Bind bundles of damp sphagnum moss around the coat hanger, securing them with the rose or floral wire, until you have a circle of moss about 3 in (7.5 cm) thick. Take the long, flexible holly branches and, using the stub wire or floral pins, wire them onto the frame in a circle. Fill the spaces with other pieces of holly and ivy, making a thick, luxuriant display.

Arrange the 8 holly-leaf fabric shapes in a circle, with their ends pointing outwards, on one of the circles of red printed fabric. Glue them into position. (If wished, you may appliqué them to the fabric instead, using a close zigzag machine stitch.) Leave the fabric until the glue is quite dry. Fold each piece of bias binding in half lengthways and then again crossways. Pin these, equally spaced, around the edge of the piece of fabric with the holly leaves on it, with the cut ends against the edge of the

16

circle. Place the two circles of fabric together, right sides inwards. Machine stitch them together around the edge, making a $\frac{5}{8}$-in (1.5 cm) seam and leaving a gap of 2 in (5 cm) for turning. Trim the seam and snip into the curves at regular intervals. Turn the circles right side out.

Fill the resulting circular bag with 'Christmas spicery' so that it becomes about $\frac{3}{8}$ in (1 cm) thick. Sew up the gap by hand. Lay the bag flat and distribute the filling evenly. Carefully and slowly machine stitch four straight lines between the holly leaves, from edge to edge of the padded circle, dividing the circle into eight equal sections.

Loop a piece of stub wire through each of the bias binding loops. Wire the circle into the centre of the wreath so that it completely fills up the space.

Coat the hook in glue. Wind the $\frac{1}{2}$-in (1.3 cm) piece of red ribbon around it to cover it, sewing down the end by hand. Depending on how the wreath is to be hung, the hook can either be left as it is or bent round to make a loop. The long piece of 2-in-wide (5 cm) ribbon can either be tied around the hook or around the hanger or knocker that is fixed to the door.

DRIED FLOWER WREATH

This is a pretty wreath, more delicate in appearance than the robust holly and ivy wreath. Hang it on an inside door.

MATERIALS

1 wire coat hanger

8-in (20 cm) length of ½-in-wide (1.3 cm) ribbon

glue for fabric

damp spaghnum moss

reel of rose or floral wire

length of Christmas beads, usually sold to decorate Christmas trees (the smaller the bead size the better)

selection of dried flowers, red, white and straw-coloured

dried green fern or asparagus leaves

12 5-in (12.5 cm) circles of a white satin-finish fabric

'Christmas spicery' (see page 114)

Bend the coat hanger into a circle, keeping the hook. Bend the hook round further so that it almost becomes a complete circle. Coat it with glue. Bind the ribbon round it, folding in the end. Sew the end of the ribbon in place if necessary. Leave to dry.

Bind spaghnum moss around the large circle made by the coat hanger and secure it with wire to make a round frame about 3 in (7.5 cm) thick.

Wind the string of beads around the frame, securing the ends to the hook with wire. Wire small bunches of dried flowers and ferns onto the frame, alternating the colours of the flowers but always keeping the greenery as the base.

Sew a line of gathering stitches round each circle of fabric 1 in (2.5 cm) from the edge. Half pull up the gathers to make a bag. Fill each bag with 'Christmas spicery.' Pull up the gathers and tie them. Use the long ends of the cotton threads to tie the bags, at regular intervals, inside the wreath.

SCENTED GARLAND

*Long, looping garlands of conifer branches give a
traditional feel to your Christmas decorations.
If they are covered in scented ornaments, they will
give a gentle fragrance to any room. The warmer
they become, the greater the fragrance, so they are at
their best in a warm living room. If you are
unable to make the garlands themselves,
you can make just the decorations to twist
onto a bought pine garland.*

MATERIALS

80-in (2 m) length of waxed
sash-cord or $\frac{1}{2}$-in (1.3 cm)
diameter flexible rope
•
small branches of pine and
fir, no more than 15 in
(38 cm) long and flexible
medium-gauge stub wire
or floral wire in 7-in
(18 cm) lengths
•
25-30 circles of shiny fabric,
each $4\frac{1}{2}$ in (11.5 cm) in
diameter (for the garland
illustrated, silver, gold and
red fabrics have been used)
•
'Christmas spicery'
(see page 114)

Lay the cord on the floor or
on a large table in the shape
in which you wish it to hang. If
the garland is to go over a
fireplace, this should be looped
upwards in the centre with the
sides hanging down in a slight
curve. You may, however, want
it to go along a ceiling beam, in
which case it can be kept
straight.

Take your evergreen bran-
ches and wire them securely
onto the cord, taking into con-
sideration the final shape. Lift
the garland up every so often to
make sure that the branches will
hang as you wish them to and
will not sag at unattractive
angles.

Make gathering stitches
around the outside of each
circle of fabric, $\frac{5}{8}$ in (1.5 cm)
from the edge. Pull up the
gathers to make small circular
bags and fill the bags with
'Christmas spicery' (each takes
about $2\frac{1}{2}$ teaspoons). Pull up
the gathers tightly and tie them
to make a soft, scented Christmas bauble. Take a piece of
wire and push it through the

neck of one of the baubles so that it sticks out by about 1½ in (4 cm). Wind the short part around the neck of the bauble to secure it. You now have a bauble on a stem of wire. Complete the others in the same way.

Using the other end of the wire, make loops for hanging the baubles at regular intervals along the garland.

Once the garland is hanging in position, the evergreen branches can be adjusted slightly and extra pieces can be added if need be.

STAIR DECORATIONS

Nothing looks more welcoming than a hallway with a decorated staircase. This raffia-based ornament helps to carry the spirit of Christmas to the upstairs rooms. When the greenery is removed on Twelfth Night (5 January), the basic decoration can be stored until the following year.

MATERIALS

strands of natural-coloured
raffia about 4 ft
(1.25 m) long
•
reel of ¼-in-wide
(6 mm) ribbon

Christmas-print fabric
•
'Christmas spicery'
(see page 114)
•
sprigs of conifer, holly
and ivy

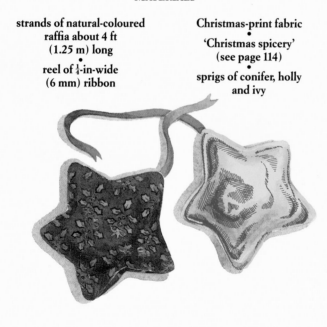

Tie 10 strands of raffia together at the top. Separate 5 of these strands and put them out of the way. Take another 10 strands of raffia, knot them together as before and tie them to the centre of the remaining 5 strands. Carry on in the same way until 5 more bundles of raffia are tied on. Take your decoration to the stairs. Tie the top knot (the one that you made first) to the top of the bannisters, tie the next knot 8 in (20 cm) down and so on, letting the free ends of raffia, that have no other bundle tied onto them, hang down. As you reach the bottom of the bannisters, add more bundles of raffia if you need them.

Now make stars for each section of raffia that hangs down. First cut 3 pieces of ribbon, 10, 15 and 20 in (25, 37 and 50 cm) long, plus 6 five-pointed stars of Christmas-print fabric, each with a 5½-in (14 cm) diameter. To make up one star, place the end of a length of ribbon on the right side of a point of one piece of fabric, with the

long tail towards the middle. Place a second piece of fabric on top so that the right sides are inwards. Taking care not to stitch across the ribbon, machine around the edge in a ¼-in (6 mm) seam, leaving a gap along the side of one point. Trim the points and clip into the corners. Turn and press the star. Fill it with 'Christmas spicery' and sew up the gap by hand. When each star is made, tie the ribbons to the raffia where the pieces are tied together. Do this for each bundle of raffia that hangs down.

Tie small sprigs of greenery onto the raffia.

SPICE RIBBONS

These spice ribbons are very delicate in appearance. The ribbons can all be the same or in contrasting colours. The spice bags illustrated were made from silver fabric, but plain red or green or a printed fabric may be used instead.

Hang the ribbons on the backs of doors, beside a fireplace, on the wall at the end of a string of cards, or on the bannister posts of stairs.

ONE SPICE RIBBON

7-in (18 cm) length of rose wire or floral wire

•

glue for the fabric

•

7 in (18 cm) of $\frac{1}{2}$-in-wide (1.2 cm) ribbon

•

3 pieces of $\frac{3}{8}$-in-wide (1 cm) or $\frac{1}{4}$-in-wide (6 mm) ribbon, measuring 13, $9\frac{1}{2}$ and $6\frac{1}{2}$ in long (32, 24 and 16 cm)

•

8 in (20 cm) of $\frac{1}{4}$-in-wide (6 mm) ribbon

THREE SPICE BAGS

3 pieces of fabric, each 8 × 2 in (20 × 5 cm)

•

3 pieces of $\frac{1}{8}$-in-wide (3 mm) ribbon, each measuring 8 in (20 cm) long

•

6 tsp 'Christmas spicery' (page 114)

Wind the wire several times to form a circle 1 in (2.5 cm) in diameter. Lightly coat this with glue. Wind the piece of $\frac{1}{2}$-in-wide (1.2 cm) ribbon around it, securing the end with a few stitches. Leave it to dry.

Place the three pieces of $\frac{3}{8}$- or $\frac{1}{4}$-in (1 cm or 6 mm) ribbon with their ends together, the shortest piece on top and the longest underneath. Put the ends of the ribbons through the prepared wire loop. Fold them over about $1\frac{1}{2}$ in (4 cm) and sew them in place with a line of stitches through all three thicknesses just below the loop. Tie the 8-in (20 cm) piece of $\frac{1}{4}$-in-wide (6 mm) ribbon in a bow over the stitches. Cut all the ends of the ribbons into V-shapes.

To make the spice bags, fold the pieces of fabric in half crossways with the right sides inside. Machine stitch along each side, allowing a $\frac{1}{4}$-in (6 mm) seam. Trim the bottom corners and turn the bags. Turn in $1\frac{1}{2}$ in (4 cm) around the top of each

bag and press. By hand run a gathering stitch round the bags 1 in (2.5 cm) below the top. Fill each bag with 2 teaspoons of 'Christmas spicery', pressing it down well. Pull up the gathers and tie them. Tie a piece of $\frac{1}{8}$-in (3 mm) ribbon round the gathers.

Hand sew the bags onto the ribbons that are hanging down from the loop, making sure that there is an equal distance between each bag as they hang down. The best method is to sew each bag's ribbon about $1\frac{1}{2}$ in (4 cm) up from the end of a hanging ribbon.

PINE CONE RIBBONS

These are made in a similar way to the spice ribbons (page 24) and can be hung in all the same places. Pine cones make an attractive, natural decoration and will look pretty simply hung from the ends of ribbons of varying lengths. Glitter paint adds a touch of sparkle and the fragrance of scented oils will last a long time.

FOR ONE RIBBON

4 7-in (18 cm) lengths of
rose wire or floral wire
•
glue for the ribbons
•
7-in (18 cm) length of
½-in-wide (1.2 cm) ribbon
•
4 pieces of ⅜-in-wide (1 cm)
ribbon measuring
4, 8, 12 and 16 in
(10, 20, 30 and 40 cm)
•
20-in (50 cm) length of
¼-in-wide (6 mm) ribbon
•
4 pine cones with opened
'petals'

silver glitter paint
•
1 tsp sandalwood oil
•
1 tsp lemon oil
•
4 4-in (10 cm) pieces of
¼-in-wide (6 mm) ribbon

Bend one piece of wire into a circle. Coat it with glue. Wind the piece of ½-in-wide (1.3 cm) ribbon around it to cover it completely, securing the ends with a few stitches. Leave it to dry.

Cut the ends of the four pieces of ⅜-in-wide (1 cm) ribbon into V-shapes. Arrange them with their ends together, the shortest piece on top and the longest underneath. Push about 1½ in (4 cm) of the ends through the loop. Sew them together just beneath the loop, going through all thicknesses. Tie the 20-in (50 cm) piece of ribbon in a bow over the stitches.

Paint each pine cone lightly with silver glitter paint. Leave them to dry. Mix the two oils together and paint them onto the cones.

Cut the ends of the 4-in (10 cm) pieces of ribbon into V-shapes. Bend a piece of wire once round and under the top layer of 'petals' of a pine cone at the stalk end. Hold one end of a piece of 4-in (10 cm) ribbon against the cone, bring the wire

round again and catch the ribbon in the wire. Fold the long end of the ribbon over the top of the pine cone and wind the wire round again, catching the second end of the ribbon under it. This will make a loop of ribbon for hanging. Sew the ribbon loops of the cones onto the lengths of ribbon that are hanging down from the wire loop.

Plaited Garlands

Garlands can be made with fabric instead of fresh greenery or dried flowers. Fill tubes of bright-coloured fabric with a spice mixture and plait them.

FOR A SINGLE GARLAND

3 strips of fabric in matching colours and patterns, each 18 in (45 cm) long × 3½ in (9 cm) wide
•
kitchen funnel

'Christmas spicery' (page 114)
•
18 in (45 cm) of ribbon, ¼ in (6 mm) wide for a straight garland; ½ in (1.3 cm) wide for a circular garland

Fold each piece of fabric in half lengthways, right side inwards, and sew a ¼-in (6 mm) seam. With this seam lying down the centre, machine stitch one end of the strip in a point. Turn the strip right side out. Cut the opposite end into a point, fold the edges inwards to make a ¼-in (6 mm) turning and press this. Press the strip flat.

Using a kitchen funnel, fill the strip with 2 tablespoons of the 'Christmas spicery' mixture. Sew up the open end by hand.

When all three strips have been filled and sewn, place them one on top of the other and pin the machined ends together across the point. Plait the strips, keeping them as flat as possible. Pin the bottom ends together across the points. Machine stitch across the points at both ends. If necessary, rearrange the plaits so that they lie evenly.

If the garland is to be used straight, take the ¼-in (6 mm) ribbon and tie one large bow at the top of the garland and one

small one at the bottom. Use a spare piece of ribbon or fabric to make a small loop for hanging and stitch it on at the back of the garland.

To make a circular garland, bend the garland in a circle, keeping the plait flat. Lay the top end over the bottom end and sew them together by hand. Rearrange the plait if necessary. Make a large, floppy bow from ½-in-wide (1.3 cm) ribbon and sew it over the join.

To make a larger hanging decoration, you will need 3 circular garlands, 28 in (70 cm) of 1½-in-wide (4 cm) ribbon and 1 wooden curtain ring.

Fold under and press ½ in (1.3 cm) at one end of the ribbon. Thread this end through the curtain ring and machine stitch it in position. Cut the other end of the ribbon into a V-shape. Sew the garlands onto the ribbon about 2 in (5 cm) apart.

CARD HOLDER

Receiving Christmas cards from friends all over the world is always a great pleasure, but finding somewhere to put them all can sometimes be difficult. This round card holder will take fifteen to twenty cards in an overlapping circle.

MATERIALS

1 circle of thick card, 14 in (36 cm) in diameter, with a 4-in-diameter (10 cm) hole cut in the centre

1 circle of thick card, 10 in (25 cm) in diameter, with a 4-in-diameter (10 cm) hole cut in the centre

1 circle of plain fabric, 15½ in (40 cm) in diameter, with a 6-in-diameter (15 cm) hole cut in the centre

1 circle of Christmas-print fabric, 13 in (33 cm) in diameter, with a 3-in-diameter (7.5 cm) hole cut in the centre

reel of cotton thread to match the printed fabric

glue for the card and fabric

'Christmas spicery' (page 114)

double-sided sticky tape, 1 in (2.5 cm) wide

Blu-Tack or similar adhesive for fixing to the wall

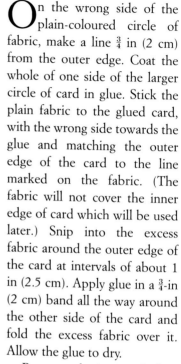

On the wrong side of the plain-coloured circle of fabric, make a line ¾ in (2 cm) from the outer edge. Coat the whole of one side of the larger circle of card in glue. Stick the plain fabric to the glued card, with the wrong side towards the glue and matching the outer edge of the card to the line marked on the fabric. (The fabric will not cover the inner edge of card which will be used later.) Snip into the excess fabric around the outer edge of the card at intervals of about 1 in (2.5 cm). Apply glue in a ¾-in (2 cm) band all the way around the other side of the card and fold the excess fabric over it. Allow the glue to dry.

Run a gathering stitch ⅝ in (1.5 cm) from the outer edge of the printed fabric. On the wrong side of the fabric, mark a line ½ in (1.3 cm) from the inner edge. Cut into this line at intervals of about ¾ in (2 cm). Position the smaller circle of card on the wrong side of the fabric with the edge of the inner circle against the marked line.

Apply glue in a ½-in (1.3 cm) band around the inner edge of the card. Fold the snipped edges of the fabric over it and leave until the glue is dry.

Lightly pull up the gathers around the edge of the fabric. Apply glue in a ¾-in (2 cm) band around one quarter of the outer edge of the card (on the same side as the previously glued band). Fold the gathers of the outer edge of fabric over the glue and leave them until the

glue has dried. Fill the gap between the card and the fabric with 'Christmas spicery'. Glue a further 3 in (7.5 cm) on each side of the first place glued, attach more of the gathered edge of the fabric and fill with more 'Christmas spicery'.

Continue in this way until you have a padded piece of card, glued and secured all round the edges. Leave it until the glue is dry.

Cut pieces of double-sided sticky tape and attach them to the inner, uncovered edge of the first piece of card. Press the padded circle on top. There will be a slit of 2 in (5 cm) between the covered circles, and the Christmas cards can simply be tucked into this.

Use Blu-Tack to fix the holder to the wall.

POTPOURRI OF THREE KINGS

One of these potpourris is golden-coloured, one contains frankincense and the other myrrh. They can be put into separate bowls and placed at various points around the room. Alternatively, you can make card containers and display them together; although the fragrance of each is distinctive, they blend very well.

MYRRH POTPOURRI

$\frac{1}{2}$ oz (15 g) larkspur flowers
•
$\frac{1}{2}$ oz (15 g) mallow flowers
•
$\frac{1}{2}$ oz (15 g) lavender flowers
•
$\frac{1}{2}$ oz (15 g) cinnamon sticks, broken
•
$\frac{1}{2}$ oz (15 g) myrrh powder
•
4 drops of cypress oil
•
4 drops of lavender oil

GOLD POTPOURRI

$\frac{1}{2}$ oz (15 g) marigolds
•
$\frac{1}{2}$ oz (15 g) yellow everlasting flowers
•
$\frac{1}{2}$ oz (15 g) camomile
•
$\frac{1}{2}$ oz (15 g) hyssop
•
1 oz (30 g) dried lemon peel
•
$\frac{1}{2}$ nutmeg, grated
•
1 tbsp orris root powder
•
4 drops of lemon oil
•
4 drops of cedarwood

FRANKINCENSE POTPOURRI

1 oz (30 g) hibiscus flowers
•
$\frac{1}{2}$ oz (15 g) peony flowers
•
$\frac{1}{2}$ oz (15 g) sandalwood chips
•
$\frac{1}{2}$ oz (15 g) dried orange peel
•
$\frac{1}{2}$ oz (15 g) frankincense powder
•
$\frac{1}{2}$ oz (15 g) cardamon pods, crushed
•
4 drops of orange oil
•
4 drops of sandalwood oil

MATERIALS FOR CONTAINERS

3 pieces of thin card
•
3 pieces of shiny, coloured paper, one gold, one red, brown or bronze, and one blue

glue
•
1 piece of thicker card
16 × 6 in (40 × 15 cm)
•
foil

If possible, make the potpourris six weeks before Christmas so that they have time to mature. Mix the ingredients for each potpourri, seal them in a plastic bag and leave for six weeks.

Note: all herbs and flowers for potpourris are dried.

To make the containers, cut out three thin card shapes following the pattern on page 117 enlarged to its full size. Score along the fold lines with the point of a pair of scissors and transfer any markings from the pattern to the card. Stick each piece of card, marked side up, onto the wrong side of a piece of coloured paper.

When the glue has dried, cut round the outside of the card with a craft knife so that the paper is cut to the exact shape. Cut round the sides and base of the legs.

On the reverse side, score along all dotted lines. Make folds away from you on score marks 1, 2, 3 and 4 and towards you on all other score marks, both horizontal and vertical. Bring flap A around to side A,

place the flap underneath the side and glue. Leave until the glue is dry. You now have a box shape. Fold in flaps B and C. Fold flap D over the top. Fold over flap E and tuck it into flap D. Stand the box on its legs. Fold in the sides in order F, G, H, I. The top part of side I will form the inside of the base of the box and none of the reverse side of the card should now be showing.

The boxes can be placed on a table without a stand, or you can cover the piece of thick card with foil and use it as a flat stand.

POMANDERS FOR CHRISTMAS

Pomanders give a delightfully old-fashioned appearance, besides a spicy scent, to your Christmas decorations. Decorate them with ribbons, arrange them in bowls or hang them in decorated net bags. Ideally, you should begin work on them in June to give them time to dry and mature. Pomanders can be made from thin-skinned oranges, lemons and limes and from firm, green, dessert apples.

FOR EACH LARGE FRUIT

1½ tbsp orris root powder
•
1½ tbsp spice mixture
•
4 drops of scented oil
•
masking tape

1 toothpick or thin knitting needle
•
1 oz (25 g) large-headed cloves
•
brown paper bag

MATERIALS FOR DECORATION

ribbons (about ½ width of masking tape)
•
cotton thread to match the ribbons

dried flowers, shiny beads or some other, small, sew-on decoration
•
net for making bags

SPICE MIXTURE FOR ORANGES

1 tbsp ground cinnamon
•
½ tbsp bayberry powder
•
4 drops of orange oil

SPICE MIXTURE FOR LEMONS

1 tbsp ground nutmeg
•
½ tbsp ground cinnamon
•
4 drops of lemon oil

SPICE MIXTURE FOR LIMES

1 tbsp ground cardamom
•
½ tbsp ground coriander
•
4 drops of lime oil

SPICE MIXTURE FOR APPLES

1 tbsp ground cloves
•
½ tbsp bayberry powder
•
4 drops of clove oil

Combine the orris root powder, spices and scented oil. If you are going to decorate your finished pomander with ribbon, bind two strips of tape to the fruit, running round from top to bottom in a cross shape. Using a toothpick or thin knitting needle, make holes in the fruit where you want to push in the cloves. Each hole should be twice the diameter of the clove head to allow for the shrinkage that takes place as the pomander matures. On pomanders that are to be displayed in a bowl or bag, you can make a simple pattern with the cloves without leaving spaces for ribbons.

When all the cloves have been pushed into the fruit, remove the tape and press the spiced mixture onto the pomander between and over the cloves. Put the pomander into a brown paper bag, together with any remaining mixture. Leave it in a cool, dry, airy place, checking its progress from time to time. When it is ready, it should sound hollow when tapped and will have shrunk considerably. The drying process may take up to six months.

To decorate the matured pomanders with ribbons, wind the ribbon around the fruit in the space left by the tape and sew the ends together underneath. Decorate the top with loops of ribbon, and dried or ribbon flowers or shiny beads.

To make a decorated net bag, cut a circle of net with a diameter four times that of the pomander. If the pomander is oval in shape (like a lemon, for example), measure its height instead of its diameter. Place the pomander in the centre of the circle and draw up the sides of the net. Mark where they meet at the top of the pomander and use thread to make a line of gathering stitches round the circle of net using the mark as a guide. Place the pomander in the net again and draw up and tie the gathers. Cut three pieces of ribbon, 25, 15 and 7 in (63, 38 and 18 cm) long. Tie the longest into a bow with the ends longer than the loops and sew it to the bottom of the net bag. Fold the smallest piece in half to make a loop and sew it to the back of the bag with the loop pointing upwards and the ends $\frac{1}{2}$ in (1.3 cm) below the line of gathers. Tie the remaining piece of ribbon around the neck of the bag with the bow on the opposite side to the loop that you have just made.

Dried Greenery Tree

In a confined space, this 'tree' can be used instead of a large Christmas tree. Stand it on a corner table near a source of warmth to make the most of the scent. Once made, the 'tree' can be carefully stored from one year to the next, but the bags of spice mixture must be renewed every year.

MATERIALS

11-in-tall (28 cm) dry
foam cone
•
6 to 8-in-long (15-20 cm)
stick about $\frac{3}{4}$ in (2 cm)
in diameter
•
block of dry foam
•
6-in-diameter (15 cm)
earthenware flower pot
•
plaster of Paris and a bowl
to mix it in
•
damp spaghnum moss

medium-gauge stub wire, cut
into 3-in (7.5 cm) lengths,
or floral pins
•
selection of dried leaves and
small flowers in varying
shades of green
•
24 pieces of Christmas-print
fabric 1½ in (4 cm) square
•
12 2½-in (6.5 cm) lengths
of $\frac{1}{8}$-in-wide (3 mm) ribbon
•
'Christmas spicery'
(page 114)

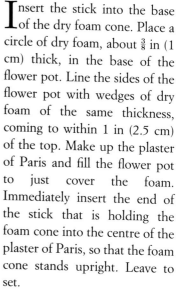

Insert the stick into the base of the dry foam cone. Place a circle of dry foam, about $\frac{3}{8}$ in (1 cm) thick, in the base of the flower pot. Line the sides of the flower pot with wedges of dry foam of the same thickness, coming to within 1 in (2.5 cm) of the top. Make up the plaster of Paris and fill the flower pot to just cover the foam. Immediately insert the end of the stick that is holding the foam cone into the centre of the plaster of Paris, so that the foam cone stands upright. Leave to set.

Bend the pieces of stub wire into U-shapes. Take small portions of spaghnum moss and, using the wire or floral pins, secure them to the cone until it is completely covered.

Cut the greenery into lengths of about 4 in (10 cm) and bind these into small bundles with wire. Working from the bottom of the cone, push these bundles into the spaghnum moss until it is completely covered.

For each decoration, fold the ribbon in half, right side out-

wards, and put the ends, facing outwards, into one corner of the right side of a square of fabric. Place another square on top so that the right sides are inwards. Machine stitch round three sides in a $\frac{1}{4}$-in (6 mm) seam. Trim the corners and turn the bag right side out. Fill it with 'Christmas spicery'. Turn in $\frac{1}{4}$ in (6 mm) at the open end and sew this up by hand. Anchor the decorations to the tree with wire or floral pins.

HANGING DECORATIONS

Scented decorations, made with dry foam and dried flowers, can be hung from beams or on hooks. Some, made in the form of a ring, can be hung against the wall or on the backs of doors.

MATERIALS

dry foam shapes such as
4-in-diameter (10 cm) balls,
bells of a similar size or
slightly larger, or 5 to 6-in-
diameter (13-15 cm) rings
•
rubberized glue or
rubber cement
•
'Christmas spicery'
(page 114)
•
ribbon for hanging

kitchen skewer
•
cinnamon sticks
•
dried flowers such as
helichrysum (straw daisies)
•
medium-gauge stub wire
or floral wire
•
scented oils (optional)

Coat the whole of the dry foam shapes in glue and roll them in the 'Christmas spicery', patting it in well so that they become completely covered and fragrant.

To calculate the length of ribbon required for the bells and globes, measure the height of the shape, multiply it by two and then add 24 in (62 cm). For the rings, measure the depth of one side of the shape, top to bottom, multiply it by two and then add 18 in (46 cm).

To insert the ribbon into the shape, fold it in half and place the ends across the top of the shape. Using a blunt skewer, gently push the ribbon through the shape until it comes out of the base. Pull both ends until they measure 6 in (15 cm) and knot them together under the shape. Cut the ends into V-shapes and let them hang down as a feature of the decoration. You will now be left with a 6-in (15 cm) loop at the top for hanging. For the rings, push the ribbon through one side in the same way and pull through 3 in

(7.5 cm). Knot the ends together and trim the ends quite short as, in this decoration, the knot will be hidden by the flowers.

The cinnamon sticks are needed for the globe and the bell. Break them into $\frac{5}{8}$–$\frac{3}{4}$-in (1.5-2 cm) pieces. Cut the wire into lengths about $1\frac{1}{2}$ in (4 cm) long and insert the wires into the pieces of cinnamon. Stick the wired cinnamon into the shape, dividing the shape into four equal sections.

Wire the flowers if necessary and use them to fill each section of the shape.

You will probably

find that the rings are too small for the cinnamon. Simply stick them all over with flowers.

If your shapes are made no earlier than two weeks before Christmas, the scent of the 'spicery' and the cinnamon will be sufficiently strong. However, if you wish to increase their scent, either soon after they are made or the following year, lightly paint the flowers with a mixture of lavender or rosemary oil and clove oils.

Store your shapes very carefully in sealed plastic bags and they will last several years.

KISSING BUNCH

*Before the Christmas tree was introduced from
Germany by Prince Albert in the nineteenth century, a
kissing bunch was the largest decoration in many
country homes. It was originally made by twisting long
branches of holly and ivy to make a large globe and
decorating this with nuts, sweetmeats and shiny
baubles. The kissing bunch was hung from the
ceiling and it was the custom for the family to kiss
underneath it on Christmas morning.*

MATERIALS

6-in-diameter (15 cm) ball of
dry foam
•
rubberized glue or
rubber cement
•
'Christmas spicery'
(page 114), or the mixture for
the Advent Calendar
(page 14)

48-in (122 cm) length of
½-in-wide (1.3 cm) ribbon
•
kitchen skewer
•
24 circles of shiny fabric
(red, silver and gold) each
3½ in (9 cm) in diameter

medium-gauge stub wire or
floral wire in 7-in
(18 cm) lengths
•
cinnamon sticks, broken
into 2-in (5 cm) lengths
•
sprigs of holly and ivy, 4 to 5 in
(10-12.5 cm) in length

Coat the ball in glue and roll it in the 'Christmas spicery' or the other mixture. Fold the ribbon in half and lay the ends over the top of the ball of foam. Using a blunt skewer, push the ribbon straight down through the ball and out of the other side. Pull about 8 in (20 cm) of both ends of the ribbon through the ball. Knot them together twice. Hold up the ball by the loop at the top. Some thinner types of ribbon may slip. If this is the case, knot the two ends of the ribbon round an empty cotton reel (thread spool). This will eventually be hidden by the holly and ivy when the decoration is finished.

Make a line of gathering stitches round the outside of each circle of fabric, $\frac{1}{2}$ in (1.3 cm) from the edge. Pull up the gathers to make small bags and fill them with your chosen scented mixture (each will take about $1\frac{1}{2}$ teaspoons). Pull the gathers tightly and knot the ends. Insert a piece of wire through the neck of each bag so that about $1\frac{1}{2}$ in (4 cm) sticks

through on the other side. Wind this end round the neck of the bag. Insert the other end of the wire through the end of a piece of cinnamon. This will give you a round bauble on the

end of a firm wire 'stalk'.

Stick sprigs of holly and ivy into the dry foam ball to cover it completely. Insert the scented baubles and cinnamon sticks between them.

Christmas Incense

Incense is often burned at religious ceremonies to increase concentration and evoke a feeling of mysticism. It is also an excellent air purifier. Burn it after Christmas dinner (and washing up!) to chase away cooking smells and also to help you to relax.

Ingredients

8 tsp sandalwood powder

1 tsp musk-scented talcum powder

2 tsp frankincense powder

1 tsp gum benzoin powder

$\frac{1}{2}$ tsp gum tragacanth powder

2 tsp liquid paraffin

10 drops each of lavender, clove and rosemary oil

$\frac{1}{4}$ tsp saltpetre dissolved in 3 tbsp water

Container

attractive bowl filled with clean sand or coloured aquarium gravel

This incense is moulded into small cones and, ideally, should be made on a bright, dry day with very low humidity. This will help it to dry out quickly and evenly.

In a bowl, mix together all the dry ingredients. Add the liquid paraffin and essential oils and begin to stir the mixture together. Add the saltpetre solution one tablespoon at a time for the first two tablespoons and then one teaspoon at a time, mixing with your fingers after each addition to ensure that the mixture sticks together well without becoming too wet. Knead the mixture with your fingers until it becomes smooth and can be rolled easily into a ball.

Have ready a wooden chopping board. Divide the incense into 32 even-sized pieces. Form each piece into a tall, thin cone shape, $1\frac{1}{4}$ to $1\frac{1}{2}$ in (3-4 cm) in height. Press the cones, wide end down, onto the board. Leave them on a sunny windowsill or in any warm, dry, airy place, for one hour. Place them on their sides and leave them for another hour. Turn them over several times during the next 24 hours. They will be completely dry when they have shrunk slightly, turned a lighter colour and feel firm to the touch when lightly squeezed.

Store the cones carefully in airtight jars or tightly sealed plastic bags, away from humidity as they can easily take in moisture.

To light the incense, fill a bowl with dry sand or aquarium gravel and into this sink the base of one, two or three cones (depending on the strength of scent required). Light the tips. The cones will burn for about fifteen minutes.

THE YULE LOG

In times gone by, when fireplaces were large enough to sit in, an enormous log called the yule log was dragged in from the woodland, decorated with evergreens, and lit on Christmas Eve. It was kept burning for the whole twelve days of Christmas and a charred fragment was kept to bring luck for a whole year and then used as tinder for the log for the following Christmas. Open fires with blazing logs are wonderful at Christmas, and this decorated log, although not nearly as big as the original yule log, will burn brightly, giving a gentle scent to the room. The best time to light it is when you have sat down to rest and talk after Christmas dinner.

MATERIALS

1 pine, apple or other sweet-smelling log about 12 in (30 cm) long and 5 to 6 in (13-15 cm) in diameter
•
waxed button thread
•
about 10 branches of bay, about the same length as the log and cut three days before use

fresh rosemary sprigs
•
paper ribbon
•
2 pine cones
•
rosemary oil
(this gives the log a stronger scent, but can be omitted if it is not available)
•
small paint brush
(if using oil)

Leaving the waxed thread on the spool, tie one end round the log. Lay a branch of bay along the log and bind the spool of thread once round it. Lay another branch of bay beside the first and wind the thread round again. Continue in the same way until the log is covered with bay leaves. Wind more thread around to secure them tightly, keeping the thread hidden as much as possible. Finally cut and tie the thread.

Tuck rosemary sprigs into the threads and when the log is well covered, tie a length of paper ribbon around the centre, finishing it off in a bow.

Paint each pine cone with rosemary oil. Tie the cones onto the top of the log with thread and add bows of paper ribbon if desired.

Before burning it, make sure you have a good fire going in the grate with other burning wood as a base. Set the log on top of the fire. As the bay leaves and rosemary begin to crackle, the scent of the herbs will mingle with that of the woodsmoke.

TREE AND TABLE

The most important Christmas decoration in many houses is the tree, resplendent in glittering decorations. Green, red, white, silver and gold are the traditional colours in which to dress the tree. A real tree, despite the needles that it drops on the carpet, is always special. Look for one that is even in shape, with masses of bushy branches, and do not bring it inside too early. It used to be thought unlucky to bring greenery into the house before Christmas Eve, but a few days before will be fine.

As soon as the tree is set up, you will notice a faint piny scent in the room. Make decorations that complement that scent and place them among the bought ones.

The table, too, becomes the centre of attention at Christmas time. Place names, napkin rings and a central decoration can all be given a subtle scent that complements your food, and crackers can be turned into scented gifts. Other tables in odd corners around the house can also have their own scented decorations and Christmas candles.

SCENTED GOLDEN ANGEL

The crowning glory of any Christmas tree is the angel on the top. If this is scented it will be even more special.

MATERIALS

1 table tennis ball

kitchen skewer

7-in (18 cm) piece of medium-gauge stub wire or floral wire

gold spray paint

gold fabric

transparent nylon thread

4½-in (11.5 cm) long cardboard tube

glue

calico

'Christmas spicery' (page 114)

6 pipe cleaners

4 2-in diameter (5 cm) circles of white net or muslin

1 yd (90 cm) silver braid

fine felt-tip pen that will write on shiny surfaces

2 twist ties

Taking one side of the table tennis ball for the face, make holes with a fine skewer in the top and bottom. Push the piece of wire through the holes. Turn back ½ in (1.3 cm) at one end and twist it to prevent the wire from slipping back through. Loop the other end round to make a halo. Spray the ball and the wire with gold paint and leave them to dry completely.

Cut a 7-in (18 cm) square of gold fabric. Join two opposite sides, right sides inwards, with a ½-in (1.3 cm) seam. Press it to one side. Turn the fabric the right way out. Fold in 1 in (2.5 cm) at one end of the resulting tube and, with the transparent thread on the outside of the tube, make a line of gathering stiches ½ in (1.3 cm) from the top of the fold.

Spread glue around the top of the cardboard tube. Slip it inside the tube of gold fabric and push it upwards until the glued rim comes to the bottom of the turning. Press the fabric onto the tube. Pull up the gathers until you have an opening on which the table tennis ball can rest. Spread glue inside the gathers, set the ball on top and leave it for the glue to dry.

Cut two wedge-shaped pieces of calico, 4 in (10 cm) wide at the top, 6 in (15 cm) wide at the bottom and 5½ in (14 cm) high. Join them together along the sides and base in a ¼-in (6 mm) seam, trim the corners and turn the bag. Half fill it with 'Christmas spicery'. Pull the bag over the bottom of the covered cardboard tube and sew it into place around the top.

To make the arms, twist the

two pipe cleaners together and bend them back $\frac{1}{4}$ in (6 mm) at each end. Place the net or muslin circles together in pairs and make gathering stitches round the edge. Pull up the gathers and put the circles over the end of the pipe cleaners like mittens. Sew them into place. Cut a strip of gold fabric 3 × 6 in (7.5 × 15 cm) and join the two long sides, right sides inwards, with a $\frac{1}{4}$-in (6 mm) seam. Turn the strip right side out and turn in $\frac{1}{2}$ in (1.3 cm) to the inside at each end. Thread the pipe cleaner arms through the strip and curve them round with the seam facing inwards. Sew the sleeves onto the mittens at the seam. Sew the arms onto the body.

For the skirt, cut a piece of gold fabric $7\frac{1}{2}$ × 16 in (19 × 40 cm). With the right sides together, join the two short sides in a $\frac{1}{2}$-in (1.3 cm) seam. Neaten this by making a zig-zag stitch through both thicknesses and press the seam to one side. Turn the fabric the right way out.

Press under $\frac{1}{4}$ in (6 mm) at the bottom and 1 in (2.5 cm) at the top. Lay silver braid around the bottom of the skirt on the outside and, using transparent thread, machine stitch through all thicknesses. Make a line of gathering stitches $\frac{1}{2}$ in (1.3 cm) from the top. Pull the skirt over the body with the seam at the back. Pull up the gathers to fit and sew the skirt into place.

For each wing, twist the ends of two pipe cleaners together to make one long piece. Twist the other ends together into a point and bend the pipe cleaners into a wing shape (see page 118). Draw round them on paper, adding $\frac{1}{2}$ in (1.3 cm) all round. Cut out the shape and use this template to cut four pieces of gold fabric. Put two pieces of fabric together, right sides inwards, and machine around the outside in a $\frac{1}{4}$-in (6 mm) seam, going round the two points but leaving a large gap. Trim the corners and turn inside out. Insert the pipe cleaner shapes into the wings and sew up the gap by hand. Sew the wings onto the angel.

Make the hair from short lengths of braid, gluing them to the head. Draw on the face. Sew the two twist ties on at the back to fix the angel to the tree.

PEG DOLLS

Peg dolls dressed in Christmas-print fabric can peep out at you from the branches of the tree. They also make ideal stocking presents.

MATERIALS

Christmas-print fabric

1 old-fashioned wooden clothes peg

calico

'Christmas spicery' (page 114)

1 pipe cleaner

½ yd (45 cm) of ⅝-in-wide (1.5 cm) lace

fine felt-tipped pens in blue and pink

black or brown four-ply knitting wool

glue for fabric and wood

13-in (33 cm) length of ⅛-in-wide (3 mm) ribbon

Cut a strip of fabric 2 × 2½ in (5 × 6.5 cm). Join the two shortest sides, right sides together, with a ¼-in (6 mm) seam. Turn the resulting tube and slip it over the peg. Turn in ½ in (1.3 mm) at the top.

Cut two wedge-shaped pieces of calico measuring 1½ in (4 cm) at the top, 3 in (8 cm) at the bottom and 3 in (8 cm) high. Join them round the sides and base in a ¼-in (6 mm) seam. Clip the corners and turn the bag. Fill it with 'Christmas spicery'. Pull it over the peg and sew it to the bodice.

To make the arms, bend the ends of the pipe cleaner towards the centre. Cut two 1-in-diameter (2.5 cm) circles of calico and run tiny gathering stitches round the edge. Pull up the gathers and slip the mittens onto the folded ends of the pipe cleaner. Sew them into place.

Cut a strip of fabric 2 × 4 in (5 × 10 cm). With the right sides together, join the two longest sides with a ¼-in (6 mm) seam. Turn the tube right side out and turn in ½-in (1.3 cm)

opening of each sleeve. Pull up the gathers to fit and sew the sleeves to the calico mittens. Sew the arms onto the body.

For the skirt, cut a piece of fabric 10 in (25 cm) wide and $3\frac{3}{4}$ in (9.5 cm) deep. With the right sides together, join the two sides with a $\frac{3}{8}$-in (1 cm) seam. Neaten this by making zigzag stitches through both thicknesses and press to one side. Turn the skirt right side out. Turn under $\frac{1}{4}$ in (6 mm) at the bottom edge and press. Pin the lace to the hem and machine stitch through both thicknesses. Turn under $\frac{1}{4}$ in (6 mm) at the top of the skirt, press it and run a gathering stitch along the edge. Slip the skirt over the body with the seam at the back. Pull up the gathers to fit and sew the skirt to the body.

Join the ends of the remaining piece of lace in a $\frac{1}{4}$-in (6 mm) seam. Gather round the top. Slip the lace over the head and pull up the gathers to fit the neck. Sew it into place.

at each end. Push the pipe cleaner arms through the tube and bend them round, with the tube seam facing inwards. Run tiny gathering stitches round the

Draw a face on the peg with the felt-tipped pens. Cut twenty 5-in (12.5 cm) lengths of wool. Tie them together in the centre. Spread glue over the top, sides and back of the head. Stick the wool 'hair' into place, spreading out the strands to fit. When the glue is dry, tie back the 'hair' with the ribbon.

FABRIC TREE DECORATIONS

Small decorations for the tree can easily be made from scraps of fabric with a Christmas print. Fill them with either 'Christmas spicery' or the 'Spiced table mixture' (both on page 114) or with the mixture that is used in the Advent calendar (page 14).

CHRISTMAS PARCELS

6 pieces of fabric, $1\frac{3}{4}$ in
(4.5 cm) square (two red,
two white, two green)
•
herb and spice mixture
for filling
•
glue for fabric
•
18 in (46 cm) of $\frac{1}{8}$-in-wide
(3 mm) ribbon

CHRISTMAS BAUBLES

2 $2\frac{1}{2}$-in-diameter (6.5 cm)
circles of fabric
•
$3\frac{1}{2}$ in (9 cm) of $\frac{1}{4}$-in-wide
(6 mm) ribbon
•
herb and spice mixture
for filling

For the **Christmas parcels**, put two pieces of the same-coloured fabric together, right sides inwards. Sew around three sides in a $\frac{1}{4}$-in (6 mm) seam. Sew the other pieces of fabric in the same way. Clip the corners and turn the fabric to make tiny bags. Turn in a $\frac{1}{4}$-in (6 mm) seam at the open end and press. Fill the bags with the herb and spice mixture and sew up the open ends by hand.

Glue the bags together in a stack, one on top of the other, and leave them until the glue is dry. Cut a piece of ribbon that will wrap around the stack of parcels with a $\frac{1}{2}$-in (1.3 cm) overlap at the base. Pin it round the parcels and sew it at the base. Wrap another piece of ribbon around the other way and sew it first to the base and then at the top.

Cut a 4-in (10 cm) length of ribbon. Slip the ends under the cross of ribbon on the top of the parcels and sew them into place to make a loop. Tie the remaining ribbon into a small bow. Sew it on top of the parcels.

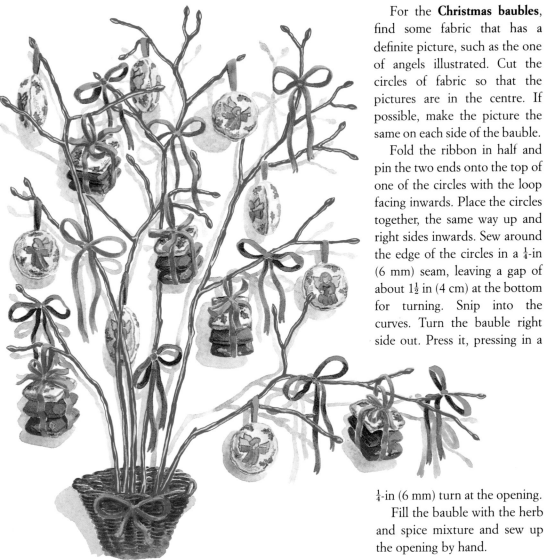

For the **Christmas baubles**, find some fabric that has a definite picture, such as the one of angels illustrated. Cut the circles of fabric so that the pictures are in the centre. If possible, make the picture the same on each side of the bauble.

Fold the ribbon in half and pin the two ends onto the top of one of the circles with the loop facing inwards. Place the circles together, the same way up and right sides inwards. Sew around the edge of the circles in a $\frac{1}{4}$-in (6 mm) seam, leaving a gap of about $1\frac{1}{2}$ in (4 cm) at the bottom for turning. Snip into the curves. Turn the bauble right side out. Press it, pressing in a

$\frac{1}{4}$-in (6 mm) turn at the opening. Fill the bauble with the herb and spice mixture and sew up the opening by hand.

DRUMS AND STARS

*Both of these decorations are made from cardboard,
one from a tube and the other from gold-covered card.*

FOR ONE DRUM

1 piece of cardboard tube,
1¾ in (5 cm) in diameter
and 1½ in (4 cm) long

•

2 circles of white fabric
2¼ in (6 cm) in diameter

•

glue for fabric and card

'Christmas spicery'
(page 114) with extra
oils added

•

1 piece of Christmas-print
fabric 6¼ × 2 in
(16 × 5 cm)

•

transparent nylon thread

•

20 in (51 cm) of narrow gold
or silver piping

FOR ONE STAR

gold-covered cardboard,
at least 9 in (23 cm) square

•

protractor

•

2 circles of silver fabric,
2½ in (6 cm) in diameter

'Christmas spicery'
(page 114)

•

1 piece of ¼-in-wide (6 mm)
ribbon, 5 in (13 cm) long

•

glue for card and fabric

For the **drum**, spread the glue in a ¼-in-wide (6 mm) band round one end of the cardboard tube, making sure that the very edge of the tube is also coated. Place a circle of white fabric over the glued end. Make snips in the edge of the fabric, about ½ in (1.3 cm) apart and fold the snipped edge down over the glue. Leave it to dry completely.

Turn the tube upside down so that the fabric is at the bottom. Fill three-quarters of the tube with 'Christmas spicery'. Cover the open end with the second piece of white fabric in the same way as the first.

Turn under and press ¼ in (6 mm) on each long side of the piece of patterned fabric. Using the transparent thread, hand-sew a length of gold or silver cord to the right side of each edge.

Fold the remaining cord in half and knot the ends together. Sew the tied ends to the inside of one long edge of the printed fabric, about one quarter of the

way along from the end.

Spread glue all over the sides of the drum. Stick the prepared printed fabric around the drum, turning in $\frac{1}{4}$ in (6 mm) at one long end as an overlap. Leave this to dry completely.

Hang the drum from the loop so that the join is out of sight.

For the **star**, draw two circles on the cardboard, each 4 in (10 cm) in diameter. Within these, draw one circle of $1\frac{1}{2}$ in (4 cm) in diameter and one circle $2\frac{1}{2}$ in (6.5 cm) in diameter. Using a protractor, draw a five-pointed star within the largest circle, using the middle circle to mark the depth of the points. Cut out the stars. Cut out the smallest circle from the centres.

Put the two circles of fabric together, right sides out. Sew small running stitches $\frac{1}{4}$ in (6 mm) from the edge, leaving a gap of 1 in (2.5 cm). Fill the resulting round bag with 'Christmas spicery'. Stitch across the gap and pull up the thread to gather the edges slightly so that when the pad of spices is laid on the star, the seam overlaps the edge of the cut-out circle.

Fold the piece of ribbon in half and glue the ends to the inside of one point of one of the card stars. Spread glue over the inside of this star. Position the pad of spices in the centre and firmly press the seam in place round the circular hole. Spread glue on the inside of the second star and position it over the first star, carefully easing the pad of spices between them. Press the stars firmly together and leave them to dry.

OLD-FASHIONED POMANDERS

Old-fashioned pomanders consisted of a perforated container filled with a strongly scented mixture of spices and herbs. Extra oils and tincture of benzoin are added to the 'spicery' mixture so that the scent floods through the holes.

FOR SIX POMANDERS

6 table tennis balls

thin skewer

6 8-in (20 cm) lengths of $\frac{1}{8}$- or $\frac{1}{4}$-in-wide (3 or 6 mm) ribbon

6 tbsp 'Christmas spicery' (page 114)

2 tsp orris root powder

2 tsp tincture of benzoin

1 tsp lavender oil

1 tsp clove oil

$\frac{1}{2}$ tsp rosemary oil

masking tape

Christmas wrapping paper (lightweight types are easier to use)

glue

clear varnish

Cut each table tennis ball in half. The easiest way to do this is to begin sawing with a bread-knife until a hole has been made in one side of the ball. The process can either be completed with the bread-knife or with kitchen snippers.

Using the skewer, make a hole through the top of one half of each ball. Fold a piece of ribbon in half and lay the ends over the hole. Using the skewer, push them through to the inside of the half-ball and knot them together. This half will then form the top of the pomander with the loop of ribbon used for hanging it.

Mix together the 'Christmas spicery', orris root powder, tincture of benzoin and oils. Fill the bottom half of each ball with this mixture.

Carefully fit the top and bottom halves together and secure them with masking tape.

Cut the wrapping paper into small pieces, $\frac{1}{2}$ to $\frac{5}{8}$ in (1.3-1.6 cm) square. You can cut these at random or select pieces that have a good colour or

pattern. Glue the squares over the outside of the pomanders in an overlapping pattern. When the pomander is completely covered you can, if you wish, cut out small, complete pictures or pieces of pattern and glue them over the random pattern. Leave the pomanders until the glue is completely dry.

Using the skewer, make holes at regular intervals all over the pomander. Hang up the pomanders and coat them in varnish. Leave them to dry completely. Open up the holes again with the skewer if necessary.

CRACKERS

These are not crackers that can be pulled. Instead, they must be unwrapped because each contains a small, pot-pourri-filled sachet that can be put into drawers and wardrobes. Use them to decorate the table or as attractively wrapped gifts.
There are two different fillings, one for men and one for women. Each amount of mixture will fill 6 crackers. The fillings must all be dried.

FOR ONE CRACKER

2 pieces of net, 6½ in (16 cm) square (use coloured or white, plain for men, patterned, if wished, for women)
•
1 piece of Christmas-print fabric, 14 × 7 in (36 × 18 cm), cut with pinking shears if possible
•
1 4½-in-long (12 cm) cardboard tube
•
glue for fabric
•
2 12-in (30 cm) lengths of ⅛-in-wide ribbon

FILLING FOR 6 CRACKERS FOR MEN

2 oz (50 g) lemon verbena leaves
•
1 oz (25 g) peppermint
•
1 oz (25 g) thyme
•
1 oz (25 g) dried lemon peel, crushed
•
1 oz (25 g) cloves, crushed
•
4 drops of lemon verbena oil
•
2 drops of clove oil

FILLING FOR 6 CRACKERS FOR WOMEN

2 oz (50 g) rose petals
•
1 oz (25 g) lavender
•
1 oz (25 g) marjoram
•
1 oz (25 g) cloves, crushed
•
4 drops of rose oil
•
2 drops of lavender oil

Lay one piece of net on top of the other and treat them as one piece. Gather 1 in (2.5 cm) on two opposite sides, starting and ending $\frac{5}{8}$-in (1.5 cm). Bring the other ends together and stitch them in a $\frac{5}{8}$-in (1.5 cm) seam. Press the seam open. Turn the resulting tubes inside out and press them again. Pull up and tie the gathers on one end. Fill each tube with the herb mixture, packing it down tightly. Pull up and tie the remaining gathers to close the tube.

Run a gathering stitch along each narrow end of the piece of printed fabric, $4\frac{1}{4}$ in (10.5 cm) from each end, starting and ending $\frac{5}{8}$ in (1.5 cm) in. Turn in and machine stitch a $\frac{1}{4}$-in (6 mm) hem on each long side.

Cut a 3-in-wide (8 cm) rectangular hole in the side of the cardboard tube, taking it to within $\frac{1}{2}$ in (1.3 cm) of each end.

Lay the cardboard tube lengthways along the centre of the wrong side of the printed fabric, with the hole facing downwards. Wrap the fabric tightly round the tube and pin the overlapping edges. Pull up and tie the gathers on each end of the tube.

Turn the cracker over so that the covered hole is facing upwards. With the point of a sharp pair of scissors pierce the centre of the hole and cut lengthways to within $\frac{1}{2}$ in (1.3 cm) of each end. Cut into the corners of the hole. Glue the flaps back into the hole.

Insert the net bag of herbs into the lined hole. Tie ribbons round the gathers on each end.

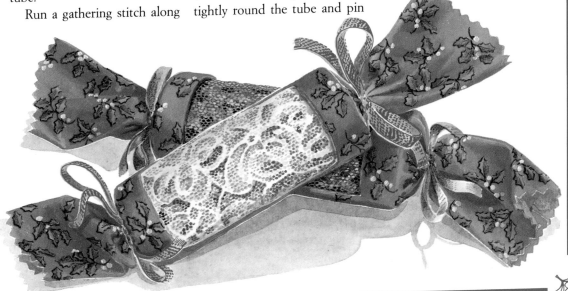

NAPKIN RINGS

To open out a clean, white napkin and release a fresh, savoury scent is a real luxury. The small bag of herb mixture is fastened to the inside of the napkin ring with a Velcro fastener so that it can be removed for washing. Being inside the ring, it will scent the napkin as well as the room. For white napkins, choose a green or red printed fabric. If you prefer dark-coloured napkins, use a white or cream print.

FOR EACH RING

1 piece of heavyweight woven interfacing 8½ × 5¼ in (21 × 13.5 cm)

•

½-in (1.3 cm) piece of Velcro fastener

1 piece of printed fabric 8½ × 5¼ in (21 × 13.5 cm)

•

1 piece of the same fabric 2 × 3 in (5 × 7.5 cm)

•

12 pieces of ric-rac braid, each 8½ in (21 cm)

•

'Spiced table mixture' (page 114)

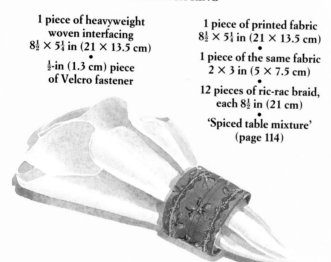

Pin the interfacing onto the wrong side of the large piece of fabric. With the right side inwards, machine stitch a ⅝-in (1.5 cm) seam, going through all thicknesses. Trim the interfacing to half the width of the seam and press the seams open. Turn the fabric right side out and press the resulting tube with the seam running down the centre instead of the side. Pin one half of the piece of Velcro fastener into the centre of the pressed strip. On the other side of the strip, make two lines of machine stitching down the centre, ¼ in (6 mm) apart and catching the Velcro fastener on the underside. Pin and machine stitch a length of ric-rac braid along each edge of the strip. Bring the ends of the strip together, right side in, and machine stitch a ⅝-in (1.5 cm) seam. Trim the seam to ¼ in (6 mm) and press it open. Hand-sew the seam to the ring at the edges to keep it flat.

Pin the other half of the piece of Velcro fastener to the centre of the right side of one

half of the small piece of fabric. With right sides together, fold the fabric in half crossways and stitch a $\frac{1}{4}$-in (6 mm) seam down each side to make a small bag. Trim the corners and turn the bag. Press the bag flat, turning in $\frac{1}{4}$ in (6 mm) at the open end. Fill the bag with the 'spiced table mixture' (it will take about 1 teaspoon) and sew up the end by hand. Fix the bag to the Velcro fastener inside the napkin ring.

PLACE NAMES

Small baskets, each with a scented filling and a name tag, give a delightful personal touch to the Christmas dinner table. With bought baskets, they are exceptionally easy to make. The small Christmas trees are a favourite with children.

BASKET PLACE NAMES

6 pieces of Christmas-print
fabric, 6 in (15 cm)
in diameter
•
'spiced table mixture'
(page 114)
•
6 small baskets

6 sprigs of alder cones
or dried berries
•
6 10-in (25 cm) lengths of
$\frac{1}{8}$-in-wide (3 mm) ribbon
•
6 plain white card tags

CHRISTMAS TREE PLACE NAMES

12 cut-out Christmas tree
shapes (page 119) in
Christmas-print fabric
•
'spiced table mixture'
(page 114)

6 4-in (10 cm) pieces of
green gardeners' cane
or any stick $\frac{1}{4}$-in
(6 mm) in diameter
•
green tissue paper
•
6 miniature flower pots
•
6 labels with string or ribbon
for tying

For the **basket place names**, make a gather around the outside of each circle of fabric, $\frac{5}{8}$ in (1.5 cm) from the edge. Pull up the gathers to make small bags and fill them with the 'spiced table mixture' (each takes about $1\frac{1}{2}$ tablespoons). Pull the gathers up tightly and tie the ends to secure them. Place each small bag in a basket with the gathers facing downwards so that they do not show. Tuck the cones or berries in beside the bags.

Punch a hole in one corner of each of the tags. Tie the lengths of ribbon onto the tags and then round the handles of the baskets.

Note: the tags can be decorated, if wished. Draw on them and colour them by hand, glue on small pictures that have been cut from old Christmas cards, or glue on dried flowers or leaves. The dried flowers can be lightly painted with scented oils, if desired.

For the **Christmas tree place names**, place the Christmas tree shapes together in twos, right sides inwards. Sew all round the outside in a $\frac{1}{4}$-in (6 mm) seam, leaving a $1\frac{1}{2}$-in (4 cm) gap in the centre of the base. Clip into the corners, turn the shapes right side out and press them.

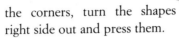

Fill the trees with 'spiced table mixture'. Push a piece of cane up through the base of each one and then sew up the gap in the stitching by hand.

Scrunch up the tissue paper and push it into each flower pot.

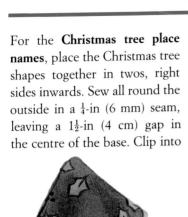

Stand the trees in the flower pots.

Write the names of each guest on the labels and tie the labels to the 'trunks' of the trees.

FINGER BOWLS

Not only are they practical, but finger bowls look pretty on the table and can give a gentle scent that blends with the aroma of the food.

MATERIALS

jug
•
dried herbs
•
sprigs or leaves of
fresh herbs
•
slices of lemon or lime
•
scented oils
•
attractive bowls in either
plain white or matching the
dinner service

Washing waters were traditionally made by boiling herbs in water and then straining it. This method gives a pleasantly scented water but it tends to be murky in colour. It is best, therefore, to pour boiling water over the herbs in a similar way to making tea. This gives a clearer, more delicate colour. If you would rather have completely colourless water, simply add scented oils to plain warm water. Decorate the bowls with sprigs or leaves of fresh herbs and thin slices of lemon or lime.

To make an infusion (tea) use 1 tablespoon of dried herbs to 30 fl oz (850 ml) of boiling water. Put the herbs into a jug, pour on the water, cover and leave for five minutes. Strain and leave until just warm. This will fill six bowls. If the scent is strong enough, simply decorate the bowls. If it needs to be slightly stronger add one drop only of the oil of the particular herb you have used.

Here are some ideas using dried herbs:

lemon verbena decorated with a slice of lemon or a twist of lemon peel and a 1-in (2.5 cm) piece of cinnamon stick;

rosemary decorated with a small fresh rosemary sprig and a slice of lemon;

peppermint decorated with a slice of lime;

lavender decorated with a few cloves and a 1-in (2.5 cm) piece of cinnamon stick;

rose petals decorated with a few cloves and a slice of lime.

Herb oils alone can be used in plain water and presented in exactly the same way as those made with fresh herbs. Oils can also be mixed in endless combinations and, if you are very clever, they will exactly blend with, or complement, the flavours of your meal. For example, if a dish is flavoured with marjoram and thyme, use a combination of marjoram and thyme oils. Use sweet, spicy oils and floral oils to complement sweet dishes and try combinations of the woodier ones such as sandalwood or cedarwood.

Allow 5 fl oz (150 ml) warm water for each dish and never add more than two drops of oil per dish. Which fresh herbs and leaves you use for decoration depends on availability. At Christmas time you should be able to pick rosemary, thyme, marjoram, winter savory, sage, lavender leaves, hyssop and the leaves of scented pelargoniums (geraniums). Also use whole cloves and all-spice berries, pieces of cinnamon and blades of mace.

Evergreen Table Decoration

This gently scented decoration can be placed in the centre of the dinner table, or on a corner table. When the candle is lit, the small, scent-filled baubles shine gently in the light.

MATERIALS

2 flexible twigs, 22 in (56 cm) long
•
2 straight twigs, 8 in (20 cm) long
•
12 straight twigs, 2½ in (6 cm) long
•
medium-gauge stub wire or floral wire in 7-in (18 cm) lengths
•
24 pine cones
•
rosemary oil
•
clove oil
•
small paint brush
•
one piece of stiff card, cut in a circle approximately 7 in (18 cm) in diameter

glue
•
'spiced table mixture' (page 114)
•
1 4½-in-diameter (11.5 cm) dry foam ball
•
12 2-in (5 cm) circles of shiny fabric (red, silver and gold were used for the decoration illustrated)
•
1 red candle, 1 in (2.5 cm) in diameter and 10 in (25 cm) high
•
24 bay leaves
•
sprigs of holly and ivy plus other evergreens such as pine or fir

Bend each long twig into a 7-in-diameter (18 cm) circle and secure it tightly with stub wire. Brace one of the circles by wiring the 8-in (20 cm) twigs to it in a cross shape. Trim the ends of the cross-pieces to fit.

Wire the short twigs at regular intervals around the outside of the braced circle so that they stand up from it. Wire the second circle to the short twigs to complete the frame. Wire the pine cones round the outside of the frame. Paint them with the scented oils.

Fit the piece of card to the inside of the frame, cutting it to fit snugly. Coat the card with glue and then cover it with 'spiced table mixture'. Leave it to dry. Cut the ball of dry foam exactly in half. Use only one half and reserve the other for another decoration. Stand the half you are using on its flat base. Using a sharp knife, cut a small hole in the centre to hold the candle. Coat the rounded part of the ball in glue and cover it with 'spiced table mixture'. Leave to dry.

To make the baubles, gather each circle of fabric $\frac{1}{4}$ in (6 mm) in from the edge. Pull up the gathers to make tiny bags and fill them with 'spiced table mixture' (each one takes about 1 teaspoon). Push a piece of the wire through the neck of each bauble so that it sticks out by about $1\frac{1}{2}$ in (4 cm). Wind the short part around the neck of the bauble.

Stand the dry foam in the prepared frame and fix the candle in the top. Put the bay leaves around the outside of the foam. Push evergreen sprigs into the foam to make a well-balanced arrangement. Push in the wired baubles, spacing them evenly.

Note: if your time before Christmas is going to be limited, you can make the framework some months in advance. Once made, it should last for several years and you can renew the scent of the pine cones every year by painting on more oils.

Dried Flower Table Decoration

This simple but highly effective decoration is best suited to an occasional table in the living room or hallway. If it is set beside a table lamp, the thin layer of glitter will catch the light.

MATERIALS

piece of bark, about 10 in (25 cm) long, from a branch about 5 in (12.5 cm) in diameter

•

Christmas-print fabric

•

'spiced table mixture' or 'Christmas spicery' (page 114)

•

toy stuffing or other suitable stuffing (e.g. shredded tights)

glue for wood and fabric

•

silver glitter paint

•

small spray of dried green foliage such as asparagus fern

•

small spray each of dried white and red flowers

•

rose or floral wire

•

20 in (51 cm) of ⅝-in-wide (1.5 cm) red ribbon

Lay the piece of bark on a table surface and measure the gap underneath the top of the bark and the table. Add 1¼ in (3 cm) to this measurement for seam allowances. Using this total measurement as a diameter, cut two circles of Christmas-print fabric. Calculate the circumference of the circles. Cut a piece of fabric of which the width equals the circumference of the circles plus 1¼ in (3 cm) for seams. The length should be the length of the piece of bark minus ¾ in (2 cm).

Join the two long sides of the fabric, right sides inwards, with a ⅝-in (1.5 cm) seam, leaving a 4-in (10 cm) gap in the middle. Press the seam open. With the right sides inwards, pin the circles into the ends of the resulting tube and stitch them into place with a ⅝-in (1.5 cm) seam. Trim the seam and turn the tube right side out. Half-fill the tube with your chosen scented mixture and on top put toy stuffing. Sew up the gap in the seam by hand.

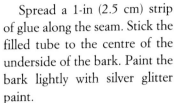

Spread a 1-in (2.5 cm) strip of glue along the seam. Stick the filled tube to the centre of the underside of the bark. Paint the bark lightly with silver glitter paint.

Lay the dried greenery along the bark and cut it to the required length and shape. With the wire, bind the red and the white flowers in separate bunches and arrange them together so that the flowers hide the wire. Bind the bunches of flowers to the sprigs of greenery towards the end of the stems. Cut the ends of the ribbon into V-shapes and tie the ribbon over the wire.

Lay the spray of flowers on the bark in the required position. Remove it and spread glue on the bark where the main parts of the spray will touch it. Press the spray gently onto the bark and leave it until the glue is completely dry.

FLOWERED CANDLE STAND

Make a stand for Christmas candles, heaped with dried flowers and surrounded by crushed cinnamon. Use dipped candles for a more natural appearance.

MATERIALS

dry foam
•
2 9-in (23 cm) candles, 1 red dipped and 1 yellow dipped
•
1 8-in (20 cm) white dipped candle
•
1 10-in (25 cm) long flat cork oval

glue
•
1 oz (25 g) cinnamon sticks
•
dried red, white and yellow helichrysum (straw daisies)
•
2 teaspoons each of lavender and clove oil

Cut three wedges of dry foam with the following dimensions: $2\frac{1}{2} \times 2$ in (6×5 cm) and $1\frac{1}{4}$ in (3 cm) thick; $2\frac{1}{2} \times 2$ in (6×5 cm) and $\frac{3}{4}$ in (2 cm) thick; $2\frac{1}{2} \times 2$ in (6×5 cm) and $\frac{5}{8}$ in (1.5 cm) thick. Trim off the corners to make elongated hexagons. Press a candle into the centre of each foam wedge to make a round mark. Using the mark as a guide, cut a small hole in each wedge to take the candle.

Place the cork base in front of you with one long side nearest you. Imagine a line across the centre from front to back. Glue the thickest piece of foam at the back, on the left-hand side of this line, the next piece in the centre of the cork on the right-hand side of the line, and the thinnest piece at the front with the main part of it on the left of the line but with one point protruding over to the right.

Break the cinnamon sticks into 1-in (2.5 cm) lengths and then crumble the lengths into thin slivers. Coat the cork base with glue. Press the cinnamon pieces onto the glue to coat the cork completely. Put the red and yellow candles into the thickest pieces of foam and the white candle into the thinnest.

Coat the top of the back piece of foam in glue and press on red flowerheads to cover it. Cover the top of the right-hand piece of foam in yellow flowers and the front piece in white. Remove the candles and then start on the sides, gluing only a small section of the foam at a time and also putting a small blob of glue on the back of each flower. Stop at regular intervals to allow the glue to dry or you will find that the flowers start to slip about. When all the pieces of foam are completely covered with flowers, leave the stand to dry for at least four hours.

Mix together the scented oils and use a small paint brush to paint the mixture onto the flowers. Put the candles back into place.

MAKING YOUR OWN CANDLES FOR CHRISTMAS

Candles for Advent and Christmas can be made in all shapes and sizes. Generally, Advent candles are white, while those for Christmas and the following days are red or green. Keep the scents warm and spicy rather than light and floral.

MATERIALS

candle moulds
•
sunflower oil or another fine cooking oil
•
wicks the right size for the moulds
•
wicking needle for rubber moulds
•
metal skewer or knitting needle
•
mould seal or Blu-Tack
•
stand for mould
•
6 oz (175 g) white beeswax
•
6 oz (175 g) paraffin wax

thermometer
•
1¼ oz (35 g) stearin (stearic acid) for glass or metal moulds or Vybar (for rubber moulds)
•
⅛ of a dye disc or colour button, grated
•
4-6 drops of candle perfume for Christmas use – bayberry, cedar, sandalwood or patchouli
•
transfers for decoration (optional) for straight-sided candles)

First choose your mould. If you are using candle perfumes, do not use plastic moulds as the perfumes damage them. Choose glass, metal or one of the many different shapes of rubber mould. The most appropriate would be a star, nativity scene, Advent or the twelve days of Christmas. Lightly oil the moulds before use.

Use a wick of the right thickness for the mould. If the mould is 1 in (2.5 cm) in diameter, you will need a 1-in (2.5 cm) wick. Push the wick through the top and into the main body of the mould. If you are using a rubber mould, you will need a wicking needle for this. Tie the wick onto a skewer and lay it across the rim of the mould. Pull the wick taut through the hole in the top of the mould and anchor it with mould seal or Blu-Tack. Cut the wick, leaving about 1 in (2.5 cm) protruding through the hole. Place the mould on a stand.

Put the beeswax and paraffin

wax into a double saucepan or into a bowl standing in a pan of water. Melt it on a low heat and bring the temperature up to 82°C (180°F). Gently melt the stearin or Vybar, together with the colour, in another saucepan. Add this to the melted wax. Add the candle perfume.

Pour the wax mixture into the moulds. If any wax is left over, keep it warm. Leave the wax in the mould for ten to twenty minutes (the larger the candle, the longer it may need). A depression will form in the centre of the wax. Carefully break the surface with a skewer and top up with the spare warm wax. Leave the candles for about five hours or until they have set completely.

Remove the mould seal. With rigid moulds, gently pull on the skewer and the candle will slip out. Rubber moulds should be carefully peeled off.

Trim the wick to about ½ in (1.3 cm).

To fix transfers onto straight-sided candles, dip the transfer in cold water for a few seconds so that the design, plus a strip of transparent paper, loosens from the backing. Place the transparent paper with the design against the candle and press it on gently with your fingers. Gently peel off the transparent paper. Smooth out any air bubbles, either with your fingers or a soft cloth. Leave the candle until the transfer is dry.

Note: this mixture makes a total volume of 15 fl oz (450 ml). Measure the amount your mould will take before beginning, by pouring in water and tipping it into a measuring jug. Make sure though that the inside of the mould is completely dry before you oil it.

ADVENT RING

In some churches, there is a tradition of lighting Advent candles on the four Sundays before Christmas. The ring is made up of four red candles, with a larger white one in the centre. On the first Sunday, one of the red candles is lit, on the second, two red candles, until, on Christmas morning, all five candles are lit. Make an Advent ring yourself using five different candle scents that complement each other so that, as Advent passes, the fragrance gradually becomes more complex. Each Sunday, light the candles for fifteen minutes.

MATERIALS

candle mould 12 in (30 cm)
high and 1 in (2.5 cm)
in diameter
•
candle mould 9 in (23 cm)
high and ¾ in (2 cm)
in diameter
•
sunflower oil
•
1 1-in (2.5 cm) and 4 ¾-in
(2 cm) wicks
•
mould seal
•
8 oz (225 g) paraffin wax
•
7 oz (200 g) white beeswax

2 oz (50 g) stearin
(stearic acid) or Vybar
(for rubber moulds)
•
metal skewers
•
⅛ red dye disc or
colour button
•
candle perfumes: bayberry,
lavender, cedar,
sandalwood, patchouli
•
1 wire coat hanger
•
5 medium-sized potatoes,
about 4 × 2 in (10 × 5 cm)
•
aluminium foil
•
sprigs of holly, ivy and pine

Read the section on candle making on page 72. Oil both moulds and put the wicks in place. Melt the beeswax and paraffin wax together. Melt the stearin in a separate pan and stir it into the wax mixture.

Pour wax into the larger mould right to the top. Add 2 drops of bayberry perfume to the wax in the mould and stir them in with a skewer. Wait for ten minutes and if a dip has appeared round the wick, top up with more wax.

Grate the red dye directly into the remaining wax mixture and warm until it has mixed in evenly. Pour coloured wax into the smaller mould. Add 2 drops of lavender candle perfume and mix them in with a skewer. Leave the candle to set, adding more wax after ten minutes if necessary. The wax in the saucepan can then be allowed to cool.

Take the smaller candle from the mould. Prepare the mould again. Gently remelt the wax in the saucepan and pour some into the mould. Add 2 drops of cedar perfume. Let the candle set, adding more wax if necessary, and repeat with the other two perfumes.

To make the ring, untwist the hook of the metal coat hanger and bend the complete piece of wire into a closed 'e' shape (a circle with a line directly across the middle). Thread the potatoes onto this shape so that one is in the centre of the cross-piece and four are equally spaced around the outside. Cut a small piece from one long side of each potato so that the potato lies flat. Scoop out a hole in the rounded side of the potato, big enough to hold a candle firmly. Cover each potato in aluminium foil. Stick sprigs of greenery into the potatoes to cover them and the frame completely. Put the white candle in the centre and arrange the red candles around it.

Note: instead of potatoes, you can use pieces of florist foam 3 × 2 in (7.5 × 5 cm) wrapped in foil.

CHRISTMAS PUDDING

*This is a rich, dark, spicy pudding that smells
wonderful as it is turned out of the dish.
It is made without suet and thus is suitable for anyone
who would rather not eat meat products. Packed
full of sweet, dried fruits, it needs only a tiny
amount of sugar.*

INGREDIENTS

2 oz (50 g) dried
whole apricots

2 oz (50 g) candied peel,
in one piece

2 oz (50 g) pitted dates

2 oz (50 g) glacé cherries

3 oz (75 g) raisins

3 oz (75 g) sultanas or
white raisins

6 fl oz (170 ml) prune juice
or red grape juice

1 oz (25 g) almonds

1½ oz (40 g) fresh,
wholewheat breadcrumbs

1½ oz (40 g) wholewheat
flour

½ tsp baking powder

¼ tsp ground allspice

¼ tsp ground ginger

¼ tsp ground cinnamon

¼ nutmeg, grated

2 tbsp soft brown
unrefined sugar

1 small cooking apple

1 medium carrot

1 egg, beaten

butter for greasing

pudding basin or mould

greaseproof paper or
baking parchment

foil

string

Finely chop the apricots, candied peel and dates and halve the glacé cherries. Mix all these in a bowl with the raisins and sultanas. Pour in the juice (prune gives a richer flavour), cover and leave for 24 hours.

Blanch and shred the almonds. Put the breadcrumbs and flour into a bowl with the baking powder, spices and sugar. Add the almonds and grate in the apple and carrot. Mix in the fruits and all the liquid that is in the bowl. Stir in the beaten egg.

Butter a 30 fl oz (850 ml) pudding basin and put in the mixture. Butter a circle of greaseproof paper or baking parchment and place it on a circle of foil. Make a pleat down the centre through both thicknesses. Place this prepared covering over the basin and tie it on with string, making a handle for easy lifting.

Fill a saucepan with water that will come about three-quarters of the way up the basin. Bring the water to the boil, lower in the pudding, cover and simmer for four hours, adding more boiling water as necessary.

Lift out the pudding and leave it for twelve hours to cool completely. Replace the covering with a fresh one. On Christmas day, boil the pudding for a further two hours.

Note: as this pudding contains very little sugar, it cannot be stored for an exceptionally long time. It will keep fresh for up to three weeks in the refrigerator. It can also be frozen.

SPICED FRUIT PUNCH

When you arrive at a party on a cold winter's night, there is nothing more welcoming than the smell of spiced punch that greets you as soon as the door is opened. Here is a recipe for a non-alcoholic punch with a rich, fruity aroma.
Put the spices needed for the spiced punch into a flagon-shaped bag to make a seasonal gift that will help to warm and cheer your friends.

FRUIT PUNCH

1 orange
•
1 lemon
•
48 cloves
•
1 apple
•
60 fl oz (1.7 ltr) red grape juice
•
20 fl oz (570 ml) pure orange juice
•
10 fl oz (285 ml) unsweetened grapefruit juice
•
2 oz (50 g) honey
•
1 piece of dried root ginger, bruised
•
1 cinnamon stick
•
½ nutmeg, grated

MATERIALS FOR A FLAGON OF SPICES

purple or deep maroon cotton or polyester/cotton fabric
•
2 strips of silver or gold fabric, 6 × 1½ in (15 × 4 cm)
•
2 lengths of gold or silver ¼-in-wide (6 mm) ribbon, 14 in (36 cm) long
•
small plastic bag for each spice
•
sheet of good-quality paper
•
4 4-in (10 cm) circles of muslin with a line of gathering stitches ⅝ in (1.5 cm) from the edge

To make the **punch**, first stick 24 cloves into both the orange and the lemon. Core the apple, leaving the peel on, and cut it into thin, lengthways slices. Put the fruit juices into a large stainless steel or enamel saucepan and add the honey, sliced fruit, gingerroot and cinnamon stick. Grate in the nutmeg. Bring the mixture to just below simmering and keep it at that temperature for ten minutes. Remove the gingerroot and cinnamon stick before serving.

To make the **flagon**, cut two pieces of purple or maroon fabric, enlarging the pattern on page 115. Put them together, right sides inwards, and machine stitch all round the sides and base of the flagon shape, ⅝ in (1.5 cm) from the edge. Trim the seam and clip into the corners and curves. Turn and press the bag. Press in ¼ in (6 mm) and then another ¼ in (6 mm) around the top of the bag. Machine stitch the turning into place.

Press under ¼ in (6 mm)

along each long side of the silver or gold strips. Press each $\frac{5}{8}$ in (1.5 cm) on one short side. With the pressed edge against the side seam, pin one of the strips across the top of the bag with its bottom edge in a line with the point where the shape begins to turn outwards. Before completing the pinning, press under the excess on the remaining short side to make the strip fit from seam to seam.

Pin the second strip to the other side of the bag. Machine stitch both strips into place along the top and bottom in one continuous line of stitching, leaving the sides open.

Thread the ribbon through the strips, one piece from each end. Overlap the ends of the ribbon and sew them together. The ribbons will now pull up to seal the bag.

Put each spice into a small plastic bag inside the flagon and include a copy of the recipe for spiced fruit punch.

SCENTED CARDS
AND GIFTS

How many times have you gone shopping for Christmas cards for the special people in your life and been unable to find exactly what you are looking for? If you make your own you will never have this problem. You can give cards that exactly suit the personality of the receiver, and you will be able to put a little bit of yourself into them too. Cards can be scented by adding padding filled with a spiced or potpourri mixture, or they can be made to form small holders for potpourri.

Gift tags, wrappings, bags, baskets and even the Christmas stocking can all be scented as can the special gifts put inside them.

Bath preparations and talcum powder can be made at home and are much cheaper, especially if you mix up a batch at a time.

Give your more practically minded friends kits so that they can make their own potpourri, cook a sumptuous meal, or brew herbal tisanes.

PADDED CARDS

What a wonderful surprise to open an envelope and take out a card that is not only good to look at but scented too! These cards have a small fabric pad filled with a scented mixture.

MATERIALS

medium-thick cardboard

•

thin cardboard, white
or coloured

•

Christmas-print fabric in two
contrasting patterns or one
plain and one patterned
(if coloured card is being
used, only one pattern of
fabric is needed)

glue for fabric and card

•

'Christmas spicery'
(page 114) or one of the
mixtures given for the gift
tags (page 86)

•

ribbon or lace for decoration
(optional)

You can either make a template for the padded cut-out or you can work with the shape of the pattern printed on the fabric. If you are making a template, you can choose the size of card that you want and make a template to fit it. If you are working with the fabric pattern, this will determine the size and shape of the card.

Generally speaking, allow about 1 in (2.5 cm) of border around the widest part of the cut-out.

Keep your cut-outs simple. A template could be in the pattern of a holly leaf, Christmas tree, bell or star (similar to those for the Advent calendar on pages 118-19, only larger). You can use a plain-coloured pad inside a patterned border or the other

way around. When using the pattern of the fabric as a guide, do not choose a complicated border pattern that would draw attention away from the pad.

If you are using your own template, draw and cut out the shape. Decide on the size of the front of the card and cut out a piece of medium-thick card to the same height and twice the width. Score it down the middle and fold it in half. Cut a piece of thin card with dimensions the same as those of the front of the folded card. Draw the template shape on the thin card and cut it out. Lay the thin card on the front of the folded card and draw round the cut shape to give a guide as to the position of the pad.

If the thin card is not coloured, cut a piece of material $1\frac{1}{4}$ in (3 cm) wider and longer than the thin card. Spread glue on the front of the thin card. Lay it with the glue against the wrong side of the fabric and smooth out any creases. Turn over the edges of the fabric and glue them back onto the card,

mitring the corners. Cut out the material from the centre of the cut-out shape, leaving $\frac{1}{4}$ in (6 mm) overlap. Trim into the curves and corners and glue back the overlap. Leave to dry. Coloured card need not be covered.

Using contrasting fabric, cut out a rough oval shape about $\frac{1}{2}$ in (1.3 cm) bigger all round than the template shape. Spread glue around the outside of three sides of the drawn shape on the folded card. Stick the fabric onto it, easing the cloth round the edges to make a bag. Fill the bag with your chosen scented filling and glue down the remaining side. Spread glue over the front of the card and also on the stuck parts of the fabric pad. Lay the thin card over the top, making sure that the filled pad comes through the cut-out shape.

If you are using the pattern of the fabric as a guide, cut a hole in the thin card $\frac{1}{4}$ in (6 mm) smaller all round than the piece of the pattern you have chosen for the pad. Mark the folded card in the same way as above. Cut out the pattern from the fabric allowing an extra $\frac{1}{2}$ in (1.3 cm) all round the piece of pattern that will make the pad. Then make up the card in the same way as above.

Ribbon bows and borders may be stuck on when the card is complete.

CARDS THAT HOLD POTPOURRI

These are cards that incorporate a small gift.
Each card stands up to make a small box on the
back that will hold potpourri.
The potpourri mixture given has a sweet, warm scent.
You can also use any of the other potpourri or spice
mixtures given elsewhere in the book.

MATERIALS	POTPOURRI FOR FOUR CARDS
thin card, preferably coloured	$\frac{1}{2}$ oz (15 g) rose petals
glue	$\frac{1}{2}$ oz (15 g) bay leaves
gold card (optional)	$\frac{1}{4}$ oz (8 g) lemon verbena leaves
glitter (if not using gold card)	1 tbsp gum benzoin powder
an old Christmas card with a small picture on it	1 tbsp orris root powder
	1 tbsp sandalwood chips
	$\frac{1}{2}$ oz (15 g) cloves, crushed
	$\frac{1}{2}$ oz (15 g) juniper berries, crushed
	2 drops each of rose, lemon verbena and sandalwood oil

Draw the star shape on page 115 to the correct size and transfer it to thin card. Cut it out. Snip at cuts 1 and 2. Score along the fold lines and fold the card back along each one.

If you are using gold card, cut out a star that is the same size as the star marked on the card. Stick it over the marked star shape on the card.

Alternatively, spread glue around the edges of the marked star and sprinkle it thickly with glitter. Leave the glue to dry and shake off any excess glitter.

Cut out a circular picture, $2\frac{1}{4}$-$2\frac{1}{2}$ in (6-7 cm) in diameter, from an old Christmas card and glue it in the centre of the star.

For ease of postage, you can send the card flat, not made up into its box shape. In this case, copy the following paragraph to send with it. 'Slip cut 1 through cut 2. Spread glue on the outside of folds 4 and 5 and tuck them inside the triangular base. You now have a triangular box into which you can empty the bag of potpourri.'

Mix the potpourri ingredients.

For each card, put one quarter of the mixture into a small plastic bag and seal it tightly.

Alternative: instead of the star shape, you can make a **candle**. Continue the lines of folds 1 and 2 upwards until each measures 6 in (15 cm) to make a candle shape. Round off the top and draw on a flame. Stick gold card or glitter over the flame. For decoration, use more glitter, stick-on stars or glitter paints, or cover the shape of the candle completely in Christmas wrapping paper.

GIFT TAGS

*Decorated gift tags always add to the attractiveness
of wrapped presents. When scented, they are
even more pleasurable.*

MATERIALS

thin card or bought gift tags
•
compasses
•
$\frac{3}{5}$-in-wide (1.5 cm)
embroidered ribbon or
plain ribbon (optional)

glue for card and fabric
•
Christmas-print fabric or
shiny fabric
•
spiced rose or herb and
spice mixture

dried flowers such as
helichrysum (straw daisies)
•
essential oils as used
for filling
•
thin ribbon or cord for ties
•
hole punch

HERB AND SPICE FILLING

1 oz (30 g) rosemary
•
2 tbsp marjoram
•
$\frac{1}{2}$ oz (15 g) lemon verbena
•
2 tbsp lavender
•
$\frac{1}{4}$ oz (7 g) cinnamon sticks,
crumbled
•
2 tbsp allspice, crushed
•
4 drops each of lavender and
lemon verbena oil

SPICED ROSE FILLING

1 oz (30 g) rose petals
•
1 tbsp sandalwood powder
•
1 tbsp cloves, crushed
•
1 tbsp juniper berries,
crushed
•
1 nutmeg, grated
•
2 drops each of rose,
sandalwood and clove oil

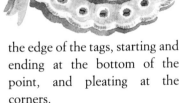

To make the tags from sheets of card, draw 2-in-diameter (5 cm) circles using compasses. Then draw a shaped top on each one that is big enough to punch a round hole through. For rectangular tags, draw rectangles 2 × 1½ in (5 × 4 cm) with a 1-in (2.5 cm) point on one side.

For the circles, cut 8-in (20 cm) lengths of ribbon. Put glue round the edge of the circle of card. Pleat the ribbon onto the glue, beginning and ending at the top and overhanging the circle all round by about ¼ in (6 mm). For the rectangles, cut 7-in (18 cm) lengths of ribbon. Glue them, without pleating, round the edge of the tags, starting and ending at the bottom of the point, and pleating at the corners.

Cut 3¾-in-diameter (9.5 cm) circles of fabric. Sew gathering stitches round the outside, ⅜ in (1 cm) from the edge. Pull up the gathers and fold in the edge to make a circle 2 in (5 cm) in diameter. Spread glue around the outside of about three-quarters of the circle, on top of the ribbon. Stick the gathered circle onto it. Fill the gathered circle with the chosen mixture. Glue the remaining part of the card circle to stick the gathered fabric down completely.

For the rectangles, cut pieces of fabric 2¾ × 2¼ in (7 × 6 cm). Press in ¼ in (6 mm) all round. Glue three sides to the back of the rectangular tag, easing them to fit. Fill the fabric with the chosen filling and glue down the remaining side.

Punch a hole through the

tops of the circles and the points of the rectangles. Tie ribbon or cord through the holes. On the plain side, glue one or two dried flowers. Paint them with similar oils to the ones used in the filling.

Bought tags can be prepared in the same way. Remember to make the circles or squares of material slightly larger than the tags so that they can be padded with the filling.

BAGS, BOXES AND WRAPPINGS

A scented wrapping can make a gift even more pleasurable. Pick a scent for the filling that suits the present and the character of the person for whom the gift is intended. Choose from the many different spice and flower mixtures in the rest of the book, such as 'Christmas spicery' or the fillings for the crackers, cards or gift tags. A word of warning, though: do not use scented wrappings for food presents as they may make them taste horrible!

BAGS

1 piece of thin card
12 × 20 in (30 × 50 cm)
•
1 piece of Christmas
wrapping paper,
12 × 20 in (30 × 50 cm)
•
glue
•
1 piece of Christmas-print
fabric or plain red or green
fabric, $6\frac{1}{2}$ × $3\frac{1}{2}$ in
(17 × 9 cm), cut with
pinking shears if possible
•
scented filling

BOXES

lidded cardboard box to fit
your present
•
Christmas wrapping paper
•
glue
•
printed or plain cotton fabric
•
scented filling

SCENTED PAPER

Christmas wrapping paper
•
essential oil
•
cotton wool/batting
•
large plastic bag

For the **bag**, coat one side of the card with glue and cover it with the Christmas wrapping paper. Draw onto it a full-size bag pattern (page 117) and cut it out. On the reverse side, so as not to mark the paper covering, score along all the fold lines. Bend the card, away from the paper covering, along all the scored lines.

Spread a $\frac{1}{4}$-in-wide (6 mm) line of glue around three sides of the card side of flap 2. Lay the piece of fabric on it, easing it to fit. Leave it for the glue to dry. Fill the resulting pad with your chosen filling. Glue the remaining side of the fabric to the card to enclose the filling.

On the outside, glue flap 4 over flap 2, and then flaps 5 and 3 over the top of both. Glue the remaining free side of the bag over the top of flap 1. Leave the bag until the glue is dry.

To cover and scent a **box**, first of all measure the box. The width of the covering paper should be the measurement across the base of the box plus four times that of the height of the sides plus 2 in (5 cm). The length should be the measurement of the height of the box plus four times the height of the sides plus 2 in (5 cm). Glue the paper to the box and trim away any corners that give a bulky appearance. The size of the covering paper for the lid can be worked out in the same way.

The scented pad can simply be placed inside the base of the box or glued inside the lid. If it is to be in the base, it is a good idea not to glue it and also to make it from fabric that is not too Christmassy. It can then be taken out and used as a drawer sachet.

For the scented pad, measure the dimensions of either the inside of the box or the inside of the lid. Cut two pieces of fabric the size of the box or lid adding $1\frac{1}{4}$ in (3 cm) to both the length and the width. Put the pieces of fabric right sides together and sew round three sides in a $\frac{5}{8}$ in (1.5 cm) seam. Trim the seam and clip the corners. Turn and press the pad. Fill with the chosen filling mixture and sew it shut. Either glue it to the inside of the lid or simply place it inside the box.

The easiest way of making a **scented wrapping** is to scent the paper itself. Put four drops of essential oil onto a small pad of cotton wool and rub it over the wrong side of the wrapping paper. Roll up the paper and seal it in a large plastic bag together with the cotton wool. Leave it for two weeks, or longer if you have time. This works better with thinner types of paper. Paper with a thick metallic surface will not take the scent so well.

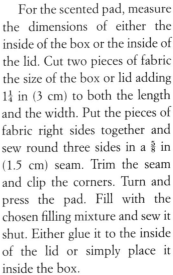

BASKETS

Some Christmas gifts – toiletries or pretty underwear, for example – look better placed in open, decorated baskets than concealed completely in a box or paper wrapping. Buy reasonably priced baskets to suit your presents and make a pretty, scented lining. Make sure that you do not use scented fillings with food.

MATERIALS

lightweight basket to suit the size and shape of your gift

•

printed cotton fabric, either with a Christmas print or a more universal design that will make the basket a lasting gift

muslin or calico

•

potpourri mixture as for the cards on page 84 (this amount will fill 4 basket liners)

•

small toy or bunch of dried flowers

Measure the diameter of the inside base of the basket. Cut two circles of printed fabric with a diameter equalling that of the base plus 1¼ in (3 cm). Cut two circles of muslin or calico the same size.

For a completely lined basket, measure the circumference of the top of the basket. Cut a strip of material equal in length to the circumference measurement plus 3 in (7.5 cm), with a width equalling the height measurement of the sides of the basket plus 1¼ in (3 cm).

For a basket with only the base lined, cut a strip of matching or contrasting fabric that is twice the circumference of the fabric circle in length and 2¼ in (5.5 cm) wide.

For either basket, put the two circles of calico or muslin together and machine stitch round the edge in a ⅝-in (1.5 cm) seam, leaving a gap of 2 in (5 cm). Trim the seam. Turn and press the resulting bag. Fill it with potpourri mixture and sew up the gap.

For the completely lined

basket, sew the ends of the strip of fabric together in a $\frac{5}{8}$-in (1.5 cm) seam. Press it open. On the top edge, press under $\frac{1}{4}$ in (6 mm) and then another $\frac{1}{4}$ in (6 mm) and machine stitch the turning into place. Make two lines of gathers on the other long edge, $\frac{5}{8}$ in (1.5 cm) and $\frac{1}{4}$ in (6 mm) in.

Pull up the gathers so that the edge of the strip fits round the circle of material. Place the strip and the circle, right sides together, with the neatened edge of the strip facing inwards. Distribute the gathers evenly and stitch in a $\frac{5}{8}$-in (1.5 cm) seam. Lay the other circle of fabric over the first, right sides together, sandwiching the gathered strip in between. Pin and sew a $\frac{5}{8}$-in (1.5 cm) seam round the edge over the top of the first stitching, leaving a gap of 2 in (5 cm). Trim the seam.

Turn and press the completed lining. Push the calico pad of potpourri into the gap. Sew up the gap by hand.

Cut two strips of fabric 1 × 15 in (2.5 × 38 cm). Press in $\frac{1}{4}$ in (6 mm) all round and press the strips in half. Machine stitch the edges together. Attach these strips by their centres, one on each side of the basket lining. Place the lining in the basket and use the strips as ties to keep it in place. Decorate the basket with a small toy or dried flowers.

For the pad to line only the base of the basket, join the two ends of the strip together in a $\frac{5}{8}$-in (1.5 cm) seam. Press it open. Press under $\frac{3}{8}$ in (1 cm) on one long side and machine stitch it. Make two lines of gathering on the other long side, $\frac{5}{8}$ and $\frac{1}{4}$ in (1.5 cm and 6 mm) from the edge. Pull them up so that the strip fits the circles of fabric. Make up the pad in the same way as the complete lining, omitting the ties as the pad will fit snugly inside the base of the basket. Again, decorate with a toy or a spray of dried flowers.

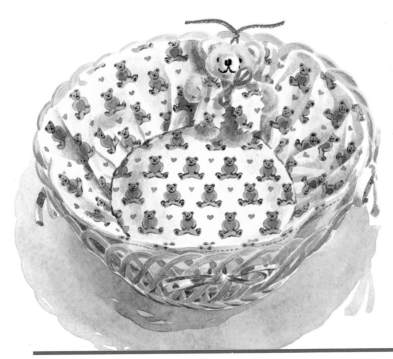

CHRISTMAS STOCKING

*A stocking bursting with small gifts is always an
exciting present for anybody, whatever their age.
Use this one as a wrapper for a special present or give it
to someone to hang up on Christmas eve. If any food
presents are going into the stocking, put them down
at the bottom, away from the scented filling.*

MATERIALS

sheet of paper for cutting
out the pattern
•
cotton fabric in two patterns
(or one plain and one
patterned) that go
together well

calico
•
potpourri mixture as for the
stand-up cards (page 84), or
any other scented mixture
such as the Advent calendar
(page 14) mix or
'Christmas spicery' (page 114)

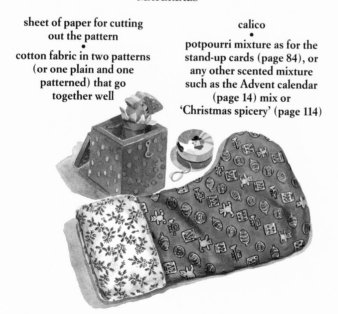

First, use the sheet of paper
to make a stocking pattern
14 in (32 cm) deep, $8\frac{1}{2}$ in (21 cm)
across the top and 11 in (28 cm)
along the foot. These measure-
ments allow for a $\frac{5}{8}$-in (1.5 cm)
seam. Cut out two stocking
shapes in printed fabric and
two in calico. For the cuff, cut
four pieces in a different fabric,
using the top $4\frac{3}{4}$ in (12 cm) of
the pattern only. Cut four pieces
of calico the same size.

With the right sides together,
join the two main pattern pieces
of printed fabric in a $\frac{5}{8}$-in
(1.5 cm) seam, leaving the top
free. Do the same with the main
pieces of calico. Trim the seams
and snip into the curves. Turn
the printed fabric stocking right
side out and press it. With the
wrong sides together, fit the
calico stocking into the printed
fabric stocking. Baste the tops
together.

Join the cuff pieces in pairs,
right sides together, making a
$\frac{5}{8}$-in (1.5 cm) seam down each
side, to form two tubes. Press
the seams open. Put the joined
cuff pieces together, right sides

in, and join them round the bottom in a ⅝-in (1.5 cm) seam. When you have trimmed the seam, turn the cuff and press it.

Press under ⅝ in (1.5 cm) around the top edge of one side of the cuff. Pin the other top edge to the top of the stocking

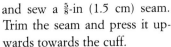

and sew a ⅝-in (1.5 cm) seam. Trim the seam and press it upwards towards the cuff.

Bring the pressed edge of the cuff to the stitching line of the seam and pin it into place at the two side seams. Make one line of machine stitching down the line of the side seams of the cuff so that the cuff is separated into two compartments.

Join the pieces of calico together in pairs, making a ⅝-in (1.5 cm) seam around three sides. Turn and press the resulting bags, pressing in ⅝ in (1.5 cm) along the unstitched ends. Fill the bags (not too full) with the chosen scented mixture. Sew up the open ends.

Insert the calico bags into the spaces in the cuff. Machine stitch the free pressed edge of the cuff to the top of the stocking, completely enclosing the calico sachets.

Fold the cuff over the stocking and press it into place so that about ½ in (1.3 cm) of the top of the cuff stays on the inside and the machine stitching remains just out of sight.

Scented Teddy Bears

Children (and adults too) love to receive a teddy as a gift. If the teddy is gently scented, it will be very special. Buy a small teddy and add your own decorations. These teddies are not suitable for babies.

Straw-hat Teddy

1 small teddy
•
straw hat to fit teddy
•
1 circle of Christmas-print fabric with diameter equal to the circumference of the hat
•
'Christmas spicery' (page 114)
•
glue for fabric

dried flowers
•
1 small basket without a handle
•
1 small piece of dry foam to fit in the basket
•
lavender oil
•
small paint brush
•
rubber band

Mop-cap Teddy

1 small teddy
•
1 circle of Christmas-print fabric with diameter equal to the circumference of the teddy's head, cut with pinking shears if possible
•
small, square muslin bag that will fit between the teddy's ears under the cap
•
'Christmas spicery' (page 114)

glue for fabric
•
1 small basket without a handle
•
1 small piece of dry foam to fit in the basket
•
dried flowers
•
lavender oil
•
small paint brush
•
rubber band

For the **straw-hat teddy**, run a line of gathering stitches round the circle of fabric, $\frac{5}{8}$ in (1.5 cm) from the edge. Pull up the gathers so that they fit exactly inside the hat crown. Half-fill the hat crown with 'Christmas spicery'. Glue the right side of the seam allowance of the fabric to the inside of the hat crown to cover and enclose the 'Christmas spicery' completely. Leave the hat until the glue is quite dry. Glue the hat to the teddy.

Coat all but the base of the dry foam with glue. Roll it in the 'Christmas spicery'. Coat the base of the dry foam with glue and stick it to the base of the basket. Cut the dried flowers with stems about 1 in (2.5 cm) long, or wire them if necessary. Push them into the dry foam to make a pretty arrangement in the basket.

Glue more dried flowers onto the teddy's hat and leave them until the glue is dry. Paint the dried flowers in both the hat and the basket with the lavender oil. Glue the basket of flowers onto the teddy's front, anchoring it with a rubber band until it is dry.

For the **mop-cap teddy**, run a gathering stitch around the circle of fabric, $\frac{5}{8}$ in (1.5 cm) from the edge.

Fill the muslin bag with 'Christmas spicery'. Sew up the end and then sew the bag onto the teddy's head, between the ears.

Pull up the gathers on the circle of fabric so that it makes a cap to fit the teddy's head. Tie the ends of the threads securely

and then glue the cap onto the teddy's head, completely covering the muslin bag.

Make and fix the flower basket in the same way as for the straw-hat teddy.

BATH OILS AND BATH VINEGARS

Fragrant preparations for adding to the bath water are always popular presents. Bath oils and bath vinegars are easy to make and their containers can be given a Christmassy look.

BATH OILS

Turkey red oil (a treated castor oil that can be bought from pharmacists and herbalists. If it is unobtainable, use almond, avocado or sunflower oil)

•

essential oils (see below)

•

suitable small bottle

•

label

BATH VINEGARS

scented herbs and flowers, fresh or dried (see below)

•

good-quality, light-coloured cider vinegar

•

spring water (if using dried herbs and flowers)

•

plastic wrap

•

suitable bottles

•

labels

First choose the right kind of bottle. For oils, it need only be small, holding about 4-5 fl oz (125-150 ml). Bath vinegars need bottles of about 16 fl oz (450 ml) capacity. The bottles can be decorated or put into containers. Hand-written, decorated labels will help to make plain bottles more attractive.

To make **bath oil**, put $2\frac{1}{2}$ fl oz (75 ml) of Turkey red oil into your chosen bottle. Add 2-$2\frac{1}{2}$ tablespoons of essential oils (see below for suggested combinations). Shake well and leave for two weeks, shaking occasionally, for the scent to mellow.

For women: 1 tablespoon each of lemon verbena and rose and $\frac{1}{2}$ tablespoon orange; $1\frac{1}{2}$ tablespoons musk and 1 tablespoon of jasmine; $1\frac{1}{2}$ tablespoons rose and $\frac{1}{2}$ tablespoon each of lavender and lemon.

For men: 1 tablespoon each of rosemary and lavender and $\frac{1}{2}$ tablespoon peppermint; 1 tablespoon each of lime and sandalwood and $\frac{1}{2}$ tablespoon of lemon.

Instructions for use (write this on a label): 'Add 1 tablespoon to the bath water.'

Scented vinegars added to the bath water act as a skin softener. They can have reviving or relaxing properties, depending on the kind of herb used. Scented vinegars can be made with either fresh or dried herbs and flowers.

To use fresh herbs, half-fill a clear glass vinegar bottle with sprigs or leaves. Fill the bottle up with vinegar, seal the top and leave it in a warm place for three weeks. Strain off the vin-

egar, pressing down well on the herbs. Bottle the liquid and leave for a week.

When using dried herbs or flowers, put 3 tablespoons of strongly scented herbs, or 6 tablespoons of delicately scented petals, into a jug. Bring 20 fl oz (570 ml) of vinegar to just below boiling point and pour it over the herbs. Cover tightly with plastic wrap and leave for twelve hours. Strain and bottle.

Suggested mixtures: 3 tablespoons of rose petals, 2 tablespoons of jasmine, $\frac{1}{2}$ tablespoon of peppermint leaves; 4 tablespoons of rose petals, 1 tablespoon of lavender flowers and 1 tablespoon of basil; 6 tablespoons of lemon verbena and 2 tablespoons of lavender flowers; 3 tablespoons of rose petals, 1 tablespoon of lemon balm and $\frac{1}{2}$ tablespoon each of basil and thyme.

Instructions for use (write this on a label): 'Add 5 fl oz (150 ml) to the bath while the taps are running.'

COLOGNES AND TOILET WATERS

Colognes and toilet waters are gifts that will give lasting pleasure throughout the year. Hunt around antique and second-hand shops to find attractive bottles.

INGREDIENTS

70 proof alcohol or a
clear, scentless vodka
•
spring water
•
herbs and flowers,
fresh or dried

whole spices
•
essential oils
•
screw-top jar
•
bottles
•
labels

Generally, a cologne is made with pure alcohol and is used more sparingly than toilet water, being dabbed on the neck, temples and wrists. Toilet water is made with alcohol and spring water and can be splashed all over the body after a bath. Both are essentially refreshing and this should be borne in mind when choosing your scented ingredients.

When using essential oils, use about 8 drops of oil to each 10 fl oz (285 ml) of alcohol or vodka, or equal quantities of alcohol or vodka and spring water. Test the oils in plain water first. You will probably develop your own favourite scents but try these combinations: orange and musk; lavender and clove; jasmine and lime; carnation, magnolia and lemon verbena.

Herbal decoctions added to alcohol or vodka make perfect **toilet waters.** Bring the herbs and 16 fl oz (450 ml) of spring water to the boil, cover and simmer for five minutes. Cool in the pan and strain, pressing down on the herbs. Mix the decoction with 10 fl oz (285 ml) of alcohol or vodka. Essential oils may also be added to increase the strength of the scent. Bottle and leave for one week. Label the bottles.

Try the following combinations of herbs and flowers (all are dried): 1 oz (30 g) lavender flowers and $\frac{1}{2}$ oz (15 g) each of lemon verbena and rosemary, adding 2 drops each of lavender and lemon verbena oil; 1 oz (30 g) each of rose petals and lavender flowers plus 1 strip of thinly pared lemon rind, adding 2 drops of rose oil and 1 drop of lavender oil; 1 oz (30 g) of rose petals and ½ oz (15 g) each of rosemary and peppermint, adding 2 drops of rose oil and 1 drop of rosemary oil.

Infusions are best for making **cologne** from undiluted alcohol or vodka. Put all the ingredients into a jar, cover tightly and shake them. Leave for three weeks, shaking every day. Strain, add more oils if required, and rebottle. Label the bottles. Since fresh ingredients are difficult to obtain in the winter months, the following recipes use dried items. All take 10 fl oz (285 ml) of vodka or alcohol:

1 oz (30 g) rose petals, 2 tablespoons of lavender flowers, 2 strips of orange rind, 1-in (2.5 cm) piece of cinnamon stick, 1 tablespoon of coriander seeds, bruised; 2 fresh rosemary sprigs or 2 tablespoons dried, 2 tablespoons of lavender, 1 tablespoon of juniper berries, crushed, 1 strip of lemon rind; 2 tablespoons of lemon verbena, 1 tablespoon of peppermint, 1 nutmeg, cut into chips, plus 2 drops of lemon verbena oil.

Talcum Powder

Talcum powder is a most useful gift and you can create special scents to suit the personality of the recipient. Make the containers from material that is not Christmassy so that they will last well into the year.

For Two Containers

3 oz (75 g) unscented talcum powder or precipitated chalk
•
3 oz (75 g) cornflour (cornstarch) or rice flour
•
½ tbsp boric acid powder or crushed crystals
•
1 tbsp orris root powder
•
1 tsp essential oil (use one type or a mixture)

Container

4½-in-long (11.5 cm) cardboard tube
•
heavy cotton fabric, such as curtain material
•
medium-weight white cardboard
•
kitchen skewer or thin knitting needle
•
label

For the **talcum powder**, mix together the dry ingredients. Add the oil drop by drop and rub it in with your fingertips until the mixture feels dry. Sieve the powder twice. Choose spicy, woody and fresh scents for men: clove, sandalwood, cedarwood, peppermint, lavender and lime; warm or floral scents with a touch of freshness for women: rose, jasmine, magnolia, musk, lemon verbena and orange.

For the **container**, cut a strip of fabric 6 in (15 cm) high and as wide as the circumference of the tube plus 1½ in (4 cm). Press under ½ in (1.3 cm) on one side and glue it. Coat the tube in glue and cover it with the fabric using the neatened edge as the overlap on the outside. Spread glue around the top and bottom and to ¾ in (2 cm) on the inside of the tube and fold in the excess fabric at the ends.

Cut two circles of cardboard of equal diameter to the ends of the tube. Cut two circles of fabric with a diameter ½ in (1.3 cm) greater. Glue the circles of card in the centres of the

underside of the covered circle to hide the glued end of the strip. Leave this hinged lid to dry.

Cut a circle of card with a diameter $\frac{1}{2}$ in (1.3 cm) greater than the diameter of the top of the tube. Using a skewer or thin knitting needle, make perforations in the centre. These are the holes through which the powder will be shaken out. On the underside score around the outside of the circle $\frac{1}{4}$ in (6 mm) from the edge. Make snips $\frac{1}{4}$ in (6 mm) apart into the line of scoring. Fold the snipped edge under. Spread glue on the fold. Insert the card into the top of the tube, easing in the fold. Use the end of a pencil to press it against the edge of the tube from inside.

Spread a little glue around the inside of the bottom of the tube and also on the right side of the excess fabric covering the remaining card circle. Using the point of a pair of fine scissors, gradually ease the glued fabric into the end of the tube until the bottom card circle fits snugly. Stand tube upright to dry.

Fill with powder and label.

wrong side of the circles of fabric. Snip at regular intervals around the overlapping fabric and glue it back over the edges of the card to give a neat circle.

Cut a strip of fabric 2 × $1\frac{1}{2}$ in (5 × 4 cm). Press the long sides to the centre on the wrong side and glue them down. Glue this strip to the inside of the top of the tube at the overlap so that the join is against the tube and half the strip is free above the tube. Leave to dry.

Glue the joined side of the free strip to the underside of one of the covered circles. Cut a circle of fabric just a fraction smaller than the diameter of the card circle. Glue it to the

BLUE DRAWER SACHETS

Drawer sachets filled with deliciously scented mixtures make ideal presents for everyone. Co-ordinate your gifts by using similar colours for male and female friends, but make them totally different in style. The shiny flowers will suit a drawer of lingerie and the denim pocket can be put among socks and sweaters.

FLOWERS

compasses
·
satin-finish fabric in both
blue and white
·
muslin or calico
·
rose-based cracker filling
(page 58) or potpourri
filling for cards (page 84)

POCKETS

denim, either lightweight or
cut from the legs of an
old pair of jeans
·
muslin or calico, for
lightweight denim only
·
herb-based cracker filling
(page 58)

To make the pattern for the **flowers**, draw a plus sign on a sheet of paper, making the two lines 9 in (23 cm) long. With the compasses draw four circles with a radius of 1½ in (3.8 cm), all meeting where the lines intersect, to give a flower shape. Add a seam allowance of ⅝ in (1.5 cm) and cut out. For the centre, cut out a 4-in-diameter (10 cm) circle.

Using the patterns, cut two flower shapes and one circle of each colour of fabric. Cut four flower shapes from the muslin or calico. Make a line of gathering stitches round the outside of the circles, ⅝ in (1.5 cm) from the edge. Pull up the gathers slightly and fold them in and press about ¾ in (2 cm) round the outside of the circles. Place a blue circle on a white flower and a white circle on a blue flower. Pin each and machine stitch it into place. Place the two blue flowers and the two white flowers together, right sides in. Machine stitch round the edge of a ⅝-in (1.5 cm) seam, leaving a gap of about 2½ in (6.5

cm). Trim the seam and clip into the curves and corners. Turn and press the flowers. Do the same with the pieces of calico or muslin. Fill the calico or muslin bags with the scented mixture and sew up the gap by machine. Put the bags inside the flowers and sew up the gap by hand.

For the **pockets**, draw a rectangle, 6 in (15 cm) across and $5\frac{1}{2}$ in (14 cm) deep. On the bottom, draw a point 2 in (5 cm) deep in the centre. Cut out this pattern and then cut out two pieces of denim. If the denim is lightweight, also cut out two pieces of muslin or calico.

Make a line of machine stitches all the way round each piece of denim, $\frac{3}{4}$ in (2 cm) from the edge and another $\frac{1}{4}$ in (6 mm) in from that. Machine stitch a motif across the pocket. Put the two pieces of denim together, right sides in. Machine stitch around the edge in a $\frac{5}{8}$-in (1.5 cm) seam, leaving a gap of about $2\frac{1}{2}$ in (6.5 cm). Trim the seam and clip across the corners. Turn and press the pocket.

If the denim is lightweight, make a muslin or calico bag in the same way. Fill it with the scented mixture, sew it up by machine and put it inside the pocket. If the denim is thick, simply fill the pocket with the mixture. Sew up the gap by hand.

PINK AND BROWN DRAWER SACHETS

DICE

protractor
·
thick, plain brown cotton
fabric, such as denim or
brushed cotton
·
plain dull pink fabric of the
same weight
·
muslin or calico
·
cracker filling (page 58) or
potpourri (page 106)

TULIPS

plain pink satin-finish fabric
·
plain brown satin-finish
fabric
·
muslin or calico
·
cracker filling (page 58) or
potpourri (page 106)

To make the pattern for the **dice**, you need to draw a cube with sides measuring $3\frac{1}{2}$ in (9 cm). To do this, take a large piece of paper and draw a horizontal line near the bottom. Using a protractor, draw a line coming up from the centre at right angles. Mark a point $3\frac{1}{2}$ in (9 cm) up this line from the first line. Draw another horizontal line at right angles from this point. From the point where the vertical line crosses the bottom horizontal line make an angle of 30 degrees on each side, using the bottom line as a base. Mark points $3\frac{1}{2}$ in (9 cm) along the lines that you have just drawn. Do the same at the top horizontal line. Join up the points on each side to make the side of the cube. Draw a horizontal line joining the top points.

From the top points on each side, make an angle of 30 degrees. The point where these lines cross marks the top of the cube. This will be the size of your finished sachet. (See diagram on page 115.) Draw lines $\frac{5}{8}$ in (1.5 cm) away from the outer line to give the seam allowance. Cut out the shape. Trace the diamond shape that makes the top of the cube. Transfer it to another piece of paper. Draw on the seam allowance and cut it out.

Cut three pieces of cotton to fit the diamond shape and one piece to fit the complete cube shape. Cut two pieces of calico or muslin to fit the complete cube shape. Join two of the diamond shapes together down one side in a $\frac{5}{8}$-in (1.5 cm) seam with the right sides inwards, leaving a gap of $\frac{5}{8}$ in (1.5 cm) at the top. Press the seam open. Join the top piece onto the bottom two pieces in the same way. Press the seam downwards.

Cut six circles of pink fabric $\frac{3}{4}$ in (2 cm) in diameter. Pin one onto the top piece, two on the right-hand section and three on the left. Appliqué them onto the fabric by hand or machine. With the right sides together and with a $\frac{5}{8}$-in (1.5 cm) seam, stitch the joined section to the complete piece, leaving a gap of about 2 in (5 cm). Trim the seam, snip the corners, turn the sachet and press it. Join the two pieces of muslin or calico together in a $\frac{5}{8}$-in (1.5 cm) seam. Trim, turn and press. Fill the calico bag with potpourri and sew up the gap by machine. Push the bag into the die-shaped sachet and sew up the gap by hand.

For the **tulip** shape, enlarge the patterns on pages 114 and 115. Cut one piece of brown satin-finish fabric and one of pink satin-finish fabric to fit the complete shape (page 115). Cut one piece of pink fabric to fit the smaller shape. Lay the small pink shape over the large brown shape and appliqué the join with machine stitching. Put the two complete shapes to-

gether, right sides in, and join them in a $\frac{5}{8}$-in (1.5 cm) seam, leaving a gap of about 2 in (5 cm). Trim the seam and clip across the corners and into the curves. Turn the sachet and press it. Make up a calico or muslin sachet in the same way, fill it with potpourri and sew up the gap by machine. Put it into the pink and brown sachet and sew up the gap by hand.

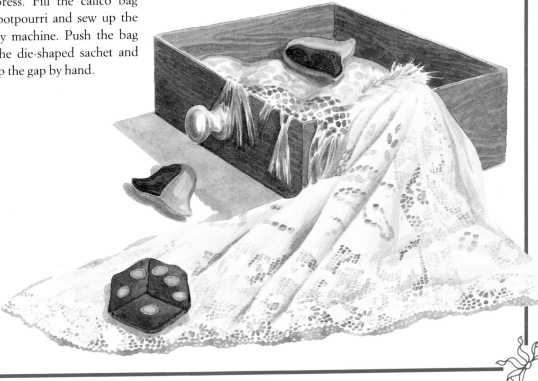

Potpourri Kit

Instead of giving a ready-made potpourri, make the present more interesting by putting together a kit that includes all the ingredients, instructions and a pretty bag that can be used later as a holder for stockings, handkerchiefs or underwear.

MATERIALS

**cotton fabric with a
floral print**

•

**2 23-in (58 cm) lengths of
$\frac{1}{2}$-in-wide (1.3 cm) ribbon,
or 2 25-in (64 cm) lengths
of cord**

•

9 small plastic bags

•

10 labels

•

**a small bottle of about 1 tbsp
(15 ml) capacity**

INGREDIENTS

1 oz (30 g) rose petals

•

**$\frac{1}{2}$ oz (15 g) lavender
flowers**

•

2 tbsp rosemary

•

2 tbsp thyme

•

2 tbsp marjoram

•

2 tbsp orange peel

•

1 tbsp cloves

•

1 tbsp allspice berries

•

1 oz (30 g) orris root powder

•

**rose, lavender and
rosemary oils**

To make the bag, cut two pieces of fabric 9¼ × 10¼ in (23.5 × 26 cm). Cut two strips 9¼ × 2¼ in (23.5 × 6 cm). Cut one strip 19 × 4¼ in (48 × 10.5 cm).

Put the two main pieces of fabric together, right sides inwards, and join them round one short and two long sides in a $\frac{5}{8}$-in (1.5 cm) seam. Clip the corners, turn the bag and press it. Put the two ends of the larger strip together, right sides facing inwards, and join them in a $\frac{5}{8}$-in (1.5 cm) seam. Trim the seam and press it open. Press the joined strip in half lengthways, right sides facing out. Run two gathering lines along the two raw edges together, $\frac{5}{8}$ in (1.5 cm) and $\frac{1}{4}$ in (6 mm) in. Pull up the gathers so that the frill fits the top of the bag. Pin and then baste it to the inside of the top of the bag, raw edges together.

Press under $\frac{5}{8}$ in (1.5 cm) along one long edge of each of the two remaining strips. Trim to $\frac{1}{4}$ in (6 mm). Press under $\frac{5}{8}$ in (1.5 cm) on each short end but do not trim. With the pressed

ends at the side seams and with the right sides inwards, pin the remaining edge of the strips over the gathered frills. Sew through all thicknesses in a $\frac{5}{8}$-in (1.5 cm) seam. Trim the seam. Bring the strips to the outside and press them into position. Machine stitch along the top and bottom of each strip, leaving the sides open.

Thread the two pieces of ribbon, from opposite ends, through the casing made by the strips. Overlap the ends by 1 in (2.5 cm) and sew them together by hand. If you are using cord, knot the ends together.

Put each of the dry potpourri ingredients into a labelled plastic bag. In the bottle, mix together 1 teaspoon of each of the oils. Label the bottle.

Write or type the following instructions: 'Mix together the flowers, herbs and orris root. Crush and add the cloves and allspice. Add six drops of the oil. Leave the potpourri in a plastic bag for one month. Put it into a bowl. Revive its scent when necessary with extra oil.'

A PRESENT OF SAVOURY SPICES

A present of culinary spices makes a lasting Christmas gift. Create an amusing case to hold them that will always look good around the kitchen.

MATERIALS

3 sheets of paper to make templates

•

brown cotton fabric, the colour of cooked pastry

•

blue or another bright-coloured cotton fabric for the 'pie dish'

•

small piece of iron-on interfacing

•

glue for fabric

•

stiff paper or thin card

8-in (20 cm) length of ¼-in-wide (6 mm) ribbon

•

small amounts of all or a selection of the following: cayenne pepper, chiles, cumin, coriander, mustard seeds, paprika, mixture of black and white peppercorns, turmeric

•

small plastic bag for each spice

•

large label for each spice

Using the pattern references on page 116, make paper templates for the three pattern pieces. To make the case, cut out two of each pattern piece, using brown fabric for the top of the pie and the coloured fabric for the dish. Put the two pieces of fabric from pattern piece 3 together, right sides inwards, and stitch a ⅝-in (1.5 cm) seam along the bottom edge. Trim the seam, turn and press. Put the two pieces of pattern piece 2 together and stitch a ⅝-in (1.5 cm) seam along the top edge. Trim the seam, turn and press.

Put the two pieces of pattern piece 1 together, right sides out. Put pattern pieces 3 on top, fitting the shapes together, and pattern pieces 2 on top of them, again matching the shape of the pieces. Sew all the way round in a ⅝-in (1.5 cm) seam. Trim, turn and press. You now have a small case with the 'crust' overlapping the top of the 'pie dish'.

Cut three small leaf shapes from the interfacing. Iron them onto some scraps of the brown fabric. Cut out the brown fabric around the leaf shapes and stick them on top of the pie.

Cut out a label from stiff paper or thin card and on it write: 'Spices for Savoury Dishes'. Thread a ribbon through it and sew it onto the pie.

Put each of the spices in a plastic bag and label each bag:

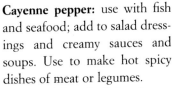

Cayenne pepper: use with fish and seafood; add to salad dressings and creamy sauces and soups. Use to make hot spicy dishes of meat or legumes.

Whole chiles: boil in vinegar for pickling; soak in oil or vinegar and crush for making hot, spiced dishes.

Cumin: use in spice mixtures, curries, stews, casseroles and rice dishes; sprinkle over lamb for roasting or grilling.

Coriander: use in spice mixture, curries, stews, casseroles and rice dishes. Add to savoury biscuits and pastries.

Mustard seeds: boil with vinegar for pickling; crush and add to marinades and sautéed dishes.

Paprika: use in sauces, soups and both meat and vegetarian casseroles and fish dishes. Add to curries; sprinkle over pizzas.

Peppercorns: grind into soups, sauces and casseroles, over meat before grilling and into vegetarian and pasta dishes.

Turmeric: use in rice dishes, curries, spiced casseroles, chicken and fish dishes. Make it a base for piccalilli.

A PRESENT OF SWEET SPICES

This is a similar gift to the savoury spice kit on the previous page. Instead of a pie dish, make a pudding shape with cream or custard on the top. Decorate the pudding with either a cherry or a holly sprig.

MATERIALS

3 sheets of paper to make templates

•

brown fabric (a textured pattern helps to give the impression of a pudding with fruit in it)

•

yellow or cream fabric

•

iron-on interfacing

•

small scrap of red fabric for the cherry or holly berry

•

scraps of green fabric for holly leaves, if making these

•

glue for fabric

•

stiff paper or thin card

ribbon

•

a selection or all of the following: whole nutmeg, ground mace, cinnamon sticks, ground cinnamon, whole cloves, vanilla pods, allspice berries, ground ginger, caraway seeds, saffron strands

•

small plastic bag for each spice

•

large label for each spice

•

8-in (20 cm) length of ¼-in-wide (6 mm) ribbon

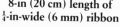

Using the pattern references on page 116, make paper templates for the three pattern pieces. To make the case, cut out two of each of the pattern pieces, using brown fabric for the main part of the pudding and yellow or cream for the topping. Put the two pieces of topping together, right sides in, and stitch along the wavy bottom edge in a $\frac{5}{8}$-in (1.5 cm) seam. Trim the seam, clip into the curves, turn and press. Put the two pieces of pattern piece 2 together, right sides inwards, and stitch across the top in a $\frac{5}{8}$-in (1.5 cm) seam. Trim, turn and press.

Put the two pieces of pattern piece 1 together, right sides outwards. Lay the custard or cream on top, matching the top edges. Lay the bottom part of the pudding on top, matching the bottom edges. Stitch round the edge in a $\frac{5}{8}$-in (1.5 cm) seam. Trim, turn and press. You should now have a case with the topping overlapping the pudding.

Cut either a holly berry and two leaves from the interfacing, or one single cherry. Iron them

onto the red and green fabric. Cut out the fabric round the edge of the interfacing. Stick the decoration onto the top of the pudding. Cut out a label from stiff paper or thin card and on it write: 'Spices for Sweet Dishes'. Thread a ribbon through it and sew it to the pudding.

On the appropriate labels, write the following information:

Allspice: add ground to cakes and biscuits, sweet puddings and fruit pies. Infuse in hot punches; grind over coffee and cream.

Caraway seeds: add to sponge cakes, sweet biscuits, sweet yeasted buns and rye bread.

Cinnamon sticks: cook with fruit, infuse in milk for puddings or in hot punch.

Ground cinnamon: add to cakes, sweet puddings and biscuits. Mix with powdered sugar and sprinkle over toast or muffins.

Cloves: cook with apples or other fruit in pies; infuse in milk for sauces and puddings; warm with ale or wine.

Ginger: add to flour for pastry or fruit for pie fillings; use to flavour cakes, puddings and biscuits; sprinkle over melon.

Mace: mix into pound cake, sponge cakes and pastry mixtures, chocolate dishes and whipped cream sweetened with honey.

Nutmeg: grate into cakes, biscuits, pancakes and yeasted buns, and over custards and junkets.

Saffron: infuse a pinch of the strands in 2 tablespoons of boiling water. Add the infusion to cakes and buns, biscuits and rich pastries.

Vanilla pod: infuse in milk or cream for puddings, custards and ice-cream. Cook gently with poached fruit. Rinse, wipe and re-use.

A PURSE OF HERBS FOR TISANES

Put a selection of herbs for making tisanes (teas) into a purse that can be used for holding packets of herbs when its original contents have been used up.

Either	Or
2 pieces of cotton printed fabric 14 in (35 cm) long and 9 in (23 cm) wide	**1 piece of natural-coloured hessian or burlap 14 in (35 cm) long and 9 in (23 cm) wide**
1 yd (90 cm) ¾-in-wide (2 cm) ribbon binding	**1 yd (90 cm) of ¾-in-wide (2 cm) ribbon binding**
1 ½-in (1.3 cm) press stud or snap	**1 ⅝-in (1.5 cm) button**
	plastic bags for the ingredients
	a sheet of good-quality paper
	herbs for tisanes (all or a selection of the following): camomile, peppermint, hibiscus, elderflowers, bergamot, lemon balm, sage, marjoram, lavender, rosemary, lime flowers

For the cotton printed fabric, put both pieces of fabric together, right sides outwards. Round off the bottom edge, making an envelope shape. Pin all round the outside of the fabric, with the heads of the pins facing inwards. Bind the top edge of the fabric, pinning the ribbon binding into place and machine stitching through all thicknesses. Fold 5 in (13 cm) of the bottom edge inwards, making a pouch with a free, rounded flap. Pin the sides together. Starting at one bottom corner, pin binding up one side of the pouch, all round the flap and down the other side of the pouch in one continuous piece, folding in the ends to neaten them. Use a press stud or snap to fasten the flap down, taking care that the stitching does not show on the right side.

For the hessian or burlap, make the pouch in the same way, using one thickness of material only. Before binding the top, make a small button loop from a short length of binding and pin it into place in the centre of the flap. Sew a button in the correct position.

Place the herbs in individual plastic bags with labels. Write the following instructions on a sheet of paper:

To make a herbal tisane: put one heaped teaspoon of dried herbs per cup into a warmed teapot. Pour on boiling water, cover and leave for five minutes. Strain into a cup. Add honey if required but not milk. Use the herbs singly or in mixtures.

Some suggested mixtures: peppermint and elderflower; camomile and lime; lavender and rosemary, bergamot and hibiscus.

APPENDIX

CHRISTMAS SPICERY

This mixture of spices and herbs is used to fill many of the items that are described in the previous pages. It has a fresh, warming scent but is never overpowering. Mix all the ingredients together and store this mixture in a sealed plastic bag until needed. After about six months you can revive it, if necessary, with extra oils.

3 oz (90 g) lavender
3 oz (90 g) cloves, crushed
1 oz (30 g) juniper berries, crushed
1 oz (30 g) bay leaves, finely crumbled
1 oz (30 g) gum benzoin powder
2 oz (60 g) orris root powder
6 drops of lavender oil
4 drops of clove oil
4 drops of lemon verbena oil

SPICED TABLE MIXTURE

Any scented decorations for the table should have a fresh, almost savoury, scent that complements rather than clashes with the food.
The following mixture uses bay and rosemary, two freshly aromatic herbs that were used to decorate banqueting halls in medieval times. The overall effect is clean, fresh and spicy. Simply mix all the ingredients together.

1 oz (30 g) lavender flowers
1 oz (30 g) rosemary
½ oz (15 g) bay leaves, finely crumbled
2 tbsp juniper berries, crushed
2 tbsp cloves, crushed
½ oz (15 g) orris root powder
4 drops of lavender oil
4 drops of rosemary oil

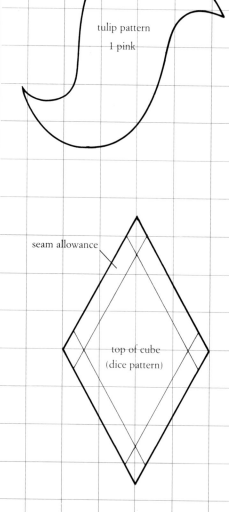

tulip pattern
1 pink

seam allowance

top of cube
(dice pattern)

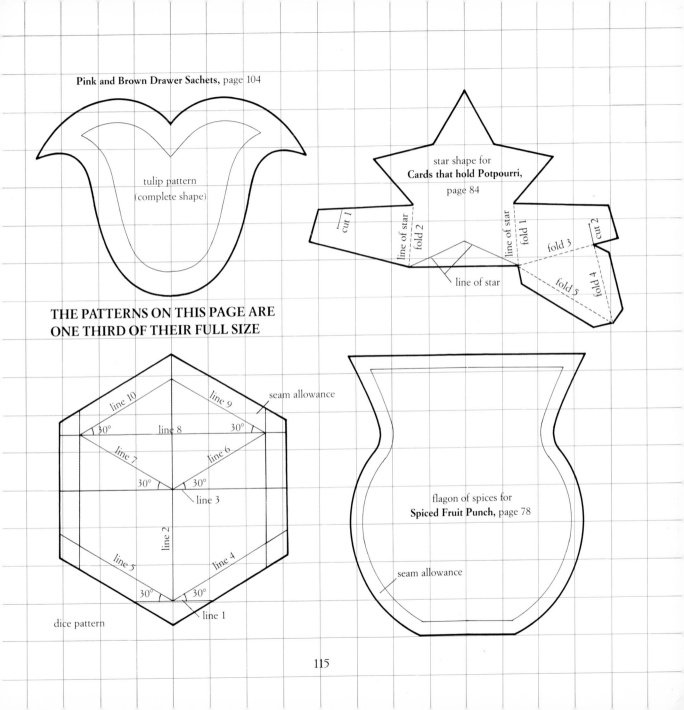

Pink and Brown Drawer Sachets, page 104

tulip pattern
(complete shape)

star shape for
Cards that hold Potpourri,
page 84

cut 1

line of star
fold 2

line of star
fold 1

fold 3

cut 2

fold 4

line of star

fold 5

THE PATTERNS ON THIS PAGE ARE
ONE THIRD OF THEIR FULL SIZE

seam allowance

line 10   line 9

30°   line 8   30°

line 7   line 6

30°   30°
line 3

line 2

line 5   line 4

30°   30°

line 1

dice pattern

flagon of spices for
Spiced Fruit Punch, page 78

seam allowance

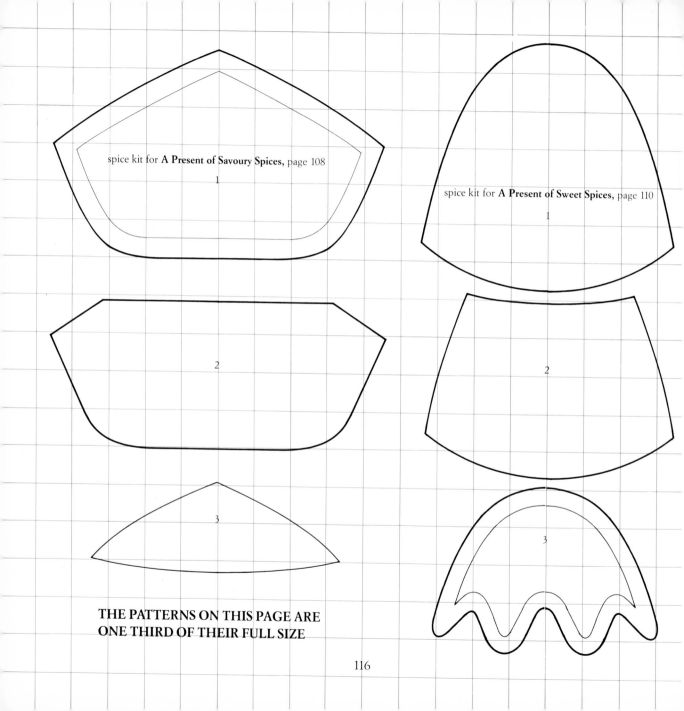

spice kit for **A Present of Savoury Spices**, page 108

1

2

3

spice kit for **A Present of Sweet Spices**, page 110

1

2

3

**THE PATTERNS ON THIS PAGE ARE
ONE THIRD OF THEIR FULL SIZE**

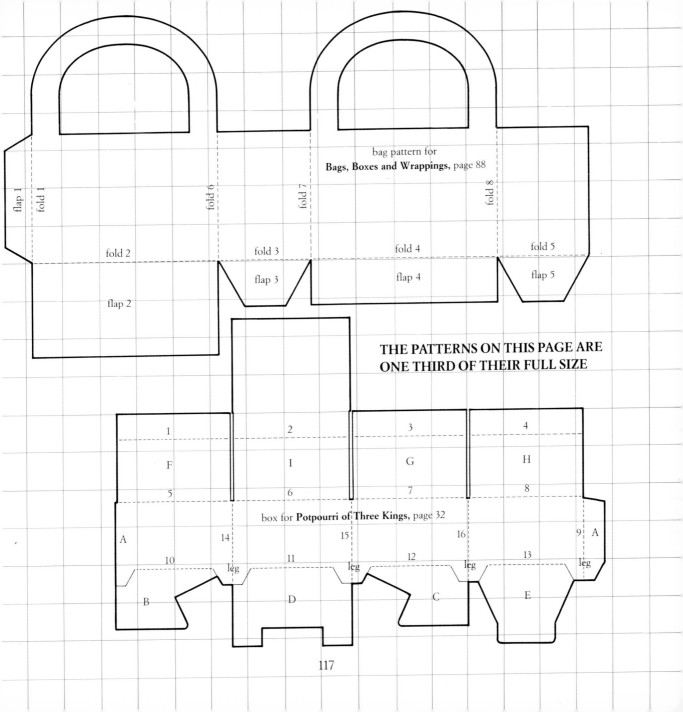

flap 1

fold 1

fold 6

fold 7

fold 8

bag pattern for
Bags, Boxes and Wrappings, page 88

fold 2

fold 3

fold 4

fold 5

flap 3

flap 4

flap 5

flap 2

**THE PATTERNS ON THIS PAGE ARE
ONE THIRD OF THEIR FULL SIZE**

| 1 | 2 | 3 | 4 |

F

I

G

H

| 5 | 6 | 7 | 8 |

box for **Potpourri of Three Kings,** page 32

A

14

15

16

9 A

| 10 | 11 | 12 | 13 |

leg

leg

leg

leg

B

D

C

E

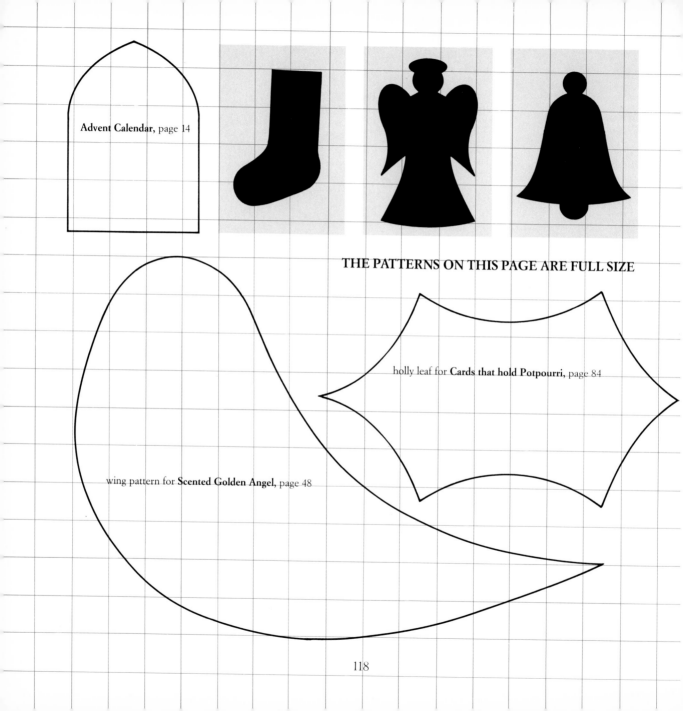

Advent Calendar, page 14

THE PATTERNS ON THIS PAGE ARE FULL SIZE

holly leaf for **Cards that hold Potpourri,** page 84

wing pattern for **Scented Golden Angel,** page 48

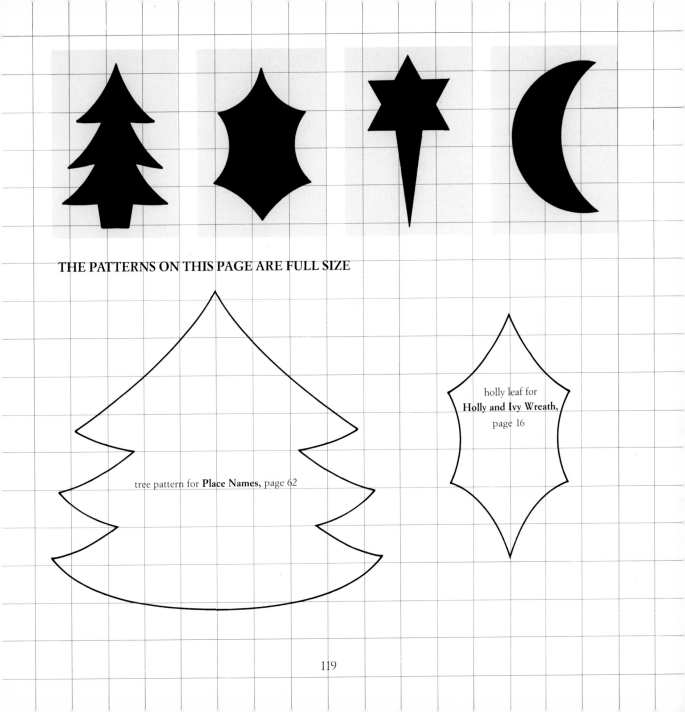

THE PATTERNS ON THIS PAGE ARE FULL SIZE

tree pattern for **Place Names,** page 62

holly leaf for
Holly and Ivy Wreath,
page 16

STOCKISTS AND SUPPLIERS

UNITED KINGDOM

All these places will supply mail order. Send a self-addressed stamped envelope for price lists.

Spices, dried herbs and flowers, woods, barks, roots, essential oils

G. Baldwin and Co.,
173 Walworth Rd, London, SE17 1RW

Pierce, A. Arnold and Son Ltd,
12 Park Road, Hackbridge, Wallington,
Surrey SM6 7ES

Candles

Candlemakers' Supplies,
28 Blythe Rd, London, W14 0HA

Herb plants and seeds

Iden Croft Herbs,
Frittenden Rd, Staplehurst, Kent,
TN12 0DH

Hollington Nurseries Ltd,
Woolton Hill, Newbury, Berks.
RG15 9XT

U.S.A. AND CANADA

Dried botanicals

Caswell-Massey Co. Ltd.
Catalog Division, 518 Lexington
Avenue, New York, NY 10017

Cherchez
862 Lexington Avenue, New York
NY 10021

Home Fragrance Stores

Crabtree & Evelyn
30 E. 67th Street, New York, NY 10021

Mail-order sources for plants, seedlings, and seeds

Alberta Nurseries & Seeds Ltd.
P.O. Box 20, Bowden, Alberta, Canada
T0M 0K0

W. Atlee Burpee Co.
300 Park Avenue, Warminster,
PA 18974

Capriland's Herb Farm
Silver Street, North Coventry CT 06238

Carroll Gardens
P.O. Box 310, 444 East Main Street,
Westminster, MD 21157

Clement Herb Farm
Route 6, P.O. Box 390, Rogers,
AR 72756

Country Manor
Route 211, Box 520, Sperryville,
VA 22740

Frog Park Herbs
RD 2, Box 151, Waterville, NY 13480

Gatehouse Herbs
98 Van Buren Street, Dolgeville,
NY 13329

Gilbertie's Herb Gardens
7 Sylvan Lane,
Westport, CT 06880

Greenfield Herb Garden
Depot & Harrison, Box 437,
Shipshewana, IN 46565

Griffin's
5109 Vickrey Chapel Road, Greensboro,
NC 27407

Hartman's Herb Farm
Old Dana Road, Barre, MA 01005

Heirloom Gardens
P.O. Box 138, Guerneville, CA 95446

The Herb Cottage
Washington Cathedral, Mount Saint
Alban, Washington, DC 20016

Herb Products Company
11012 Magnolia Blvd., P.O. Box 898,
N. Hollywood, CA 91601

Hilltop Herb Farm
P.O. Box 325, Romayor, TX 77368

Hoo Shoo Too Herb Farm
20261 Hoo Shoo Too Road, Baton
Rouge, LA 70817

Maine Balsam Fir Products
P.O. Box 9, West Paris, ME 04289

Earl May Seed & Nursery
208 North Elm, Shenandoah, IA 51603

Meadowbrook Herb Garden
Route 138, Wyoming, RI 02898

Meadowsweet Herb Farm
729 Mount Holly Road,
North Shrewsbury, VT 05738

Merry Gardens
P.O. Box 595, Camden, ME 04843

Nature's Herb Company
1010 46th Street, Emeryville, CA 94608

New York Botanical Gardens
Southern Blvd. at 200th Street, Bronx,
NY 10458

Old Sturbridge Village
1 Old Sturbridge Village Road,
Sturbridge, MA 01566

Park Seed Co.
P.O. Box 46, Greenwood, SC 29647

Plants of the Southwest/Seeds
1570 Pachebo Street, Santa Fe,
NM 87501

Richters
Goodwood, Ontario LOC 1A0, Canada

St. John's Herb Garden
7711 Hill Meade Road, Bowie,
MD 20720

The Sassafrass Hutch
11880 Sandy Bottom, NE, Greenville,
MI 48838

Shady Hill Garden
821 Walnut Street, Batavia, IL 60510

Sinking Springs Herb Farm
234 Blair Shore Road, Elkton,
MD 21921

Smile Herb Shop
4908 Berwyn Road, College Park,
MD 20740

Stillridge Herb Farm
10370 Route 99, Woodstock, MD 21163

Thompson and Morgan, Inc.
Jackson, NJ 08527

Tom Thumb Workshops
P.O. Box 322, Chincoteague, VA 23336

Wayside Gardens
Hodges, SC 29695

Well-Sweep Herb Farm
317 Mt. Bethel Road, Port Murray,
NJ 07865

Whipple House Mail Order
76 Otis Street, Westborough, MA 01581

White Flower Farm
Litchfield, CT 06759

NEW ZEALAND

Hillside Herbs Ltd.
166 Fairy Springs Road, Rotorua
(073) 479 535

Floriste Addingtown
292 Lincoln Road, Addington,
Christchurch
(03) 384 017

Gail's Floral Studios
Centreplace, Victoria Street, Hamilton
(071) 393 758

AUSTRALIA
NEW SOUTH WALES

The Fragrant Garden
25 Portsmouth Road, Erina NSW 2250
(043) 67 7322

The Lavender Patch
Lot 3, Cullens Road, Kincumber
NSW 2250
(043) 68 1233

H.E. Koch & Co Pty Ltd
1 Probert Street, Camperdown
NSW 2050
(02) 519 8044

Dural's Colonial Cottage & Gallery
62 Kenthurst Road, Dural NSW 2158
(02) 654 1340

Roy H Rumsey Pty Ltd
P.O. Box 1, 1335 Old Northern Road,
Dural NSW 2158
(02) 652 1137

Swanes Nursery
490 Galston Road, Dural NSW 2158
(02) 651 1322

Argyle Soap & Candle Co.
33 Playfair Street, The Rocks
NSW 2655
(02) 241 3365

Common Scents Herb Cottage
745 Old Northern Road, Dural
NSW 2158
(02) 651 1027

Aguis Phillip
Suite 67, 61 Marlborough Street,
Surrey Hills NSW 2010
(02) 690 1703

The Flower Warehouse
Cnr Barney and Castle Streets, North
Parramatta NSW 2150
(02) 630 7466

VICTORIA

Ring of Roses
90 Maling Road, Canterbury Vic 3126
(03) 836 2814

Potpourri & Sachet Supplies
P.O. Box 53, Northcote Vic 3070
(03) 489 8405

Coora Cottage Herbs
Thompsons Lane, Merricks Vic 3916
(059) 89 8338

The Gumleaf Candle Co.
No 80, Mangans Road, Lilydale
Vic 3755
(03) 735 3755

Australian Botanical
68 Burwood Road, Hawthorn Vic 3122
(03) 818 2673

QUEENSLAND

Ahisma
Drivers Court, Cobble Creek Qld 4523
(07) 289 9191